THE NEW ENGLISH GRAMMAR:
A DESCRIPTIVE INTRODUCTION

THE NEW
ENGLISH GRAMMAR:

A Descriptive Introduction

N. R. CATTELL
with a Foreword by Wayne O'Neil

THE MIT PRESS
Cambridge, Massachusetts, and London, England

CONTENTS

FOREWORD

I

In the pages that follow, I will not comment at all on
the substance and presentation of linguistic theory in
Mr. Cattell's book except to say straightaway that it is
an admirably clear and concise presentation of a sub-
stantial theory of language and of the main features of
English grammar. There is no need to recapitulate
here what the book itself does so well. Rather, I will
deal with a topic that Mr. Cattell alludes to but, since
this was not his purpose, does not dwell on: the conse-
quence of such a theory for and its role in general education.

For many long years, grammar study has lain at the
heart of the school curriculum: in the schools of America there are certainly, at any one moment of the study
day, more children toiling over grammar than over all
else combined. Yet few ask whether grammar should
continue to be central and, if so (perhaps even if "may-
be"), then why. At a time when highly commercial
publishers and publicly financed curriculum produc-
tion centers (both mining the new-found curricular

talents of the university "experts") are cram-jamming modern linguistics into the school day, it is especially important to consider these questions thoughtfully, rationally, and carefully.† Too often in today's highly bureaucratized educational system, decisions of basic importance to education are made for reasons unrelated to the proper goals of education; they are made instead on the basis of whether, for example, the materials are multimedia, modern, teacher-proof, routinized, automated, or sequentialized. It would be pleasant if such important decisions about what to teach, what course to follow, what set of texts (if any) to adopt, and so on, could for once be based on knowledge, on a concern for achieving a good education, on noncommercial honesty. This can be the case only if people in education, educators and laymen alike, read books like Mr. Cattell's and then consider seriously their possible educational consequences. It is to reflections of this sort that I now turn.

II

Public compulsory education exists, on the one hand, in order that the myths of the dominant culture may be properly transmitted to and reinforced in all the members of the society. On the other hand, a proper and important goal of education is that children come to understand how to construct coherent explanations

---

†For an extensive discussion of some of the same issues raised here and for a critical examination of one of the new linguistics textbook series, see my "'Paul Roberts' Rules of Order: The Misuses of Linguistics in the Classroom," *Urban Review* 7.2:12–16 (June 1968). A few of the following paragraphs have in fact been adapted from that article.

(formal and informal) of data—that they learn to generalize significantly across facts. It is presumably in this way that new directions through the real world are seen and perhaps followed, and that career choices and intellectual decisions are not foreclosed. There are, of course, other educational goals, but I believe that these two predominate in educational theory and practice.

Now the second of these goals is very often perverted when the aim becomes rote learning of generalizations (perhaps even of outdated ones) rather than coming to them through discussion and hard work around facts. Worse though, the two goals become badly confused when the data are so limited and chosen that the rote-learned generalizations attempting to explain them are in fact the myths of the culture. Look no further than the standard textbook treatment of American history (the settling of the West, the Civil War, America in the Philippines, etc.) to see that the myth generalizations dished up there are simply not consonant with the full range of facts available.

Now it is only where myths are at stake that such confusion can arise, only there that the contradictory nature of these goals becomes so obvious that relentlessly pursuing the latter is destructive of ever achieving the former. (Counterfactual beliefs about physical forces carry no weight in a physics classroom, while claims about the importance of Shakespeare to everyman can find neither rational confirmation nor disconfirmation.) And this is certainly a proper ordering of affairs: cultural myths deserve to survive (if at all) only insofar as they stand up to the challenge of the full range of data. The image of a jolly, good-willed, peace/democracy/have-not-loving Uncle Sam should survive only if in fact it is a true image: we must know what we are if we are ever to become what we would want to be.

All of this seems far off from language and grammar, I hear you cry. Not really, for there are significant and far-reaching myths about language and especially about language differences that prevail in America (and in most other countries). Consider, for example,

1. That there exists a standard language that is systematic and "logical" and beside it unsystematic and less logical substandard language(s).
2. That the unsystematic and illogical nature of substandard language is a function of the generally (morally) depraved ways of the lower classes.

These myths appeal immediately and in fact make a major contribution to an individual's paranoid belief in the imperfectability of humankind, and in this way their effect is quite the opposite of American historical myths that lead one on to complacency and self-satisfaction. For they attack some aspect of an individual's social identity, lead to social insecurity, and are, in fact, totally destructive of school talk, of intergroup talk, and so on.

Now if language were to be studied in the schools in the way, for example, that the physical universe is studied, that is, in an objective, scientific way, with no attention given to mindless myth, with due consideration of the facts of language, no support whatsoever for the language myths would ever emerge. For there is none. Arguments for the systematic and supposedly

more logical character of preferred ways of speaking/
writing would melt away as the systematicity and logic
(whatever this could mean) of less preferred ways of
speaking/writing became clear — in fact, dialects would
differ in trivial ways only. And socioeconomic class explanations as well as climatic and physiological (folk)
explanations of language differences would have to be
given up as geographical and historical factors were
brought forth. In other words, the existing myths could
hardly emerge from (even quite informal) consideration of the facts of language.

It is important that these myths be destroyed, for
clearly they are part of racist and elitist beliefs that a
proper education should work toward erasing rather
than sustaining. That education was in origin elitist is a
sad enough fact, but that it should continue to promul-
gate elitism while going public and compulsory is
intolerable.

Erasing the myths that surround language or, better,
providing no support for them would simply be a by-
product of attempting to generalize across language
data or perhaps of drawing certain conclusions from
the generalizations. From this point of view, language
study would play an important role in a very general
goal: arriving at coherent, rational explanations of the
human differences, class differences, their naturalness,
and so on. It is, of course, another matter entirely to
argue that language study can contribute importantly
to the general goal of theory construction, that it is
proper grist for the mills of coherent discussion. Is
there something about language that makes it especially amenable to this sort of examination? Clearly
there is: the availability of the data to be explained.

In some new science and math curriculums there are attempts to get children to discover the generalizations that account for an array of data. There are, however, great difficulties, for children can bring very little of themselves to bear on such problems. The problems must then be tightly packaged so that the possibility of error, of making a wrong discovery, is eliminated or at least minimized. By carefully constraining the data made available, the student is led toward the foregone conclusion. The claim is that this is inductive teaching and that learning is "doing" science.

This is hardly better than rote-learning generalizations and considerably more wasteful of time. Surely "doing" science is quite another thing: theories are not built up inductively out of data, nor do they emerge from a poor acquaintance with the data. Thus it is clearly a mistake to teach the ways of science in a poor context. For such learning must go on in a context that is rich and full, one to which the child has some immediate access.

Such an area is language. A speaker of a language has a knowledge of it in a way that he has knowledge of few other things. The knowledge is, to be sure, tacit, but it can be tapped in ways that his knowledge of American history, say, cannot be until he is filled full of the facts of American history. Moreover, in grammar there are no unchallenged or unchallengeable explanations: the teacher does not and cannot hold the secret in his back pocket.

I can thus imagine, and in fact have run classes of this sort myself, a legitimate and important classroom activity being grammar construction. To various levels of precision and formality, a class can proceed to come up with significant generalizations, a consistent set of them accounting for the complex array of English sentences and for the intuitions that speakers of the language have about the structure of sentences and relationships among them. Thus grammar does not become a procrustean bed of *do*s and *don't*s into which sentences must be rudely forced; but rather the grammar must be made to fit the facts. Language study can then be, in part, the writing of a grammar of a class's own language with considered attention to any individual differences that are uncovered. What is finally learned will possibly be of far more general significance than any set of generalizations upon English sentences, which can only prove wrong on closer examination anyway. What is learned is theory construction itself, how to come to grips with the problem of offering consistent, coherent explanations of complex arrays of data. And this is an area where the learner has some knowledge and access to potentially limitless data: there he can gain insight into the nature of formal explanations and formal systems.

III

The goals of grammar and language study just sketched in bear interesting relationships to the traditional goals: "On a single point, at least, all English grammarians are united," wrote Alonzo Reed and Brainerd Kellogg in 1878. "They hold that, by the study of grammar, the pupil should acquire the art of using the English language with propriety. A study of the science that does not issue in this, all agree, fails of its proper end."† Clearly, one of the goals of grammar study has always been to improve oral and written expression, to get children to speak and write better. Now much can depend on such a term as "better," and much does. To speak and write better in the world of rhetoric – in that corner of the English class – is simply to be in tune with what is deemed effective and polished and sweet speaking/writing in one's own time – at least in the time of one's teachers. To speak and write better in grammar in that corner is simply to try nervously to cover up one's social and/or regional origins, to sound and write middle-class, or rather the way the middle class imagines itself to speak and write. Now whether we consider these goals laudable or ludicrous, happy or hallucinatory – and it should be obvious that I consider them tragic – a straightforward question is whether the study of grammar can in any way help in realizing them.

It is certainly easy to understand why it was believed to be a help, for when such goals were formulated, the school population was significantly an immigrant population that literally did not speak English; moreover in the not-too-distant past, education had simply meant education through a language not one's own (through Latin, for example). The prevailing method of teaching a foreign language being the grammar-translation method, what was more logical than pummeling the children with parsing, diagrams, and rules?

And so the teachers did. Yet there was never any reason to believe that grammar should be effective. After all, foreign language teaching never took very

†*An Elementary English Grammar* (New York, 1878), p. 3.

well. And now, in fact, because a great deal of re-
search energy has been spent on such questions (albeit
much of it very badly designed research), it is clear
that the extent of a young man's knowledge of formal
grammar relates at least as well to his skill at pool as it
does to his ability to express himself in speech and
writing. There is nothing in research or in logic to lead
us to believe it should be any different. For grammar
comprehends such a small piece of language – and
nothing of language use – that no designs for "im-
provement" could at all follow from it. Worse, of
course, is that though we have some intuitive sense,
for example, about what good writing is, we have no
ways whatsoever of objectifying that goodness. Why
then should objective knowledge of grammar lead to
improving we know not exactly what?

Faced with this dilemma, Reed and Kellogg would
probably have us give up the enterprise. Yet the nine-
teenth century had another (very vaguely defined) goal
for grammar study: it provided mental discipline.
That's what I think it's all about, too. And in the preceding section I have essentially tried to give a somewhat precise characterization of "mental discipline."
Language study is not important for what it finally allows one to do with language; it is important for the
questions it asks and the freedom it opens up to one in
answering them.

Wayne O'Neil

Cambridge, Massachusetts
February 1969

PREFACE

This book is an attempt to provide students, teachers, and other interested people with an account of English grammar which will be in step with the knowledge provided by modern linguistics, and yet will be comprehensible to readers with no specialized linguistic training. It has been a difficult aim to pursue, for the translation of rigorously expressed technical material into the language of common communication holds the same difficulties and dangers as any other kind of translation. There is a ceaseless conflict between the need to be accurate and the need to be clear, and compromises have to be made on many occasions. Nevertheless, I would like to think that this book will be a useful preliminary for any students who wish to proceed later to the more demanding study of grammar through linguistics.

No one can write a book about present-day grammatical knowledge, it seems to me, without using the brilliant work of Noam Chomsky, the American scholar who has revolutionized linguistics, and with it the study of English grammar; but numerous other scholars have also contributed work of immense value, and some of their names will be found in the bibliography. My debt to their insights is enormous.

I wish to express my gratitude to my wife, Jill, for clerical and other help, and for her forbearance during the writing of the book. My grateful thanks are also due to Mr. Nicholas Hudson, the Manager for Australia of Heinemann EducationalBooks Limited, who first suggested the writing of the book, and who has given me wonderful freedom to produce it in my own way and my own time.

N. R. Cattell

University of Newcastle
New South Wales, Australia
July 1966

THE NEW ENGLISH GRAMMAR:
A DESCRIPTIVE INTRODUCTION

1
GRAMMAR
OLD AND NEW

1.1 GRAMMAR: A NASTY EXPERIENCE

When I was a pupil in the sixth grade of the primary school, grammar lessons were exciting and terrifying events. The six-foot headmaster would brandish what seemed like a six-foot cane, write a very hard sentence on the board, underline some words, and point at someone with the electrifying command: *Parse!* And how we did parse! One hesitation, or one mistake, and we were "out." We soon became very skillful at this game, and were very seldom wrong. And, in some ways, despite the dangers, it was a richly satisfying pastime —for those who were successful. No doubts disturbed us: we were either right or wrong, "safe" or "out." The grammar book had something of the awesome infallibility of the Bible. Others have had similar experiences in their early training in grammar, and if their abilities did not happen to coincide with those required for this eccentric game, they now look back on their classroom experience of grammar as a nasty one.

Not only was grammar nasty, it was also dull. Even quite bright people found it uninteresting in itself.

There were many tedious items to learn, and if you learned them all, you would no doubt become as dull as grammar teachers or the writers of grammar books, but fortunately you could get through life without knowing many of them.

The strange thing was that many of the people who had secretly decided that grammar was not for them nevertheless believed that right and wrong in grammar were as separate as black and white. As adults, they may sometimes be uncertain which is the correct form of a sentence, but they are never uncertain that there *is* a correct form. They are deeply convinced of the existence of inflexible rules, which they could learn if they were not too lazy.

However, in the last twenty or thirty years, a revolution has taken place in the academic approach to grammar. Not only is the difference between grammatical black and white not regarded as absolute; there are even many eminent linguists who would refuse to apply the terms "right" and "wrong" to language at all. Not only is the parsing I learned at school not infallible; nearly every aspect of it has been brought into question and looked at critically. And grammar, instead of being a dead subject, with all its facts compiled for all time, has become part of the lively young social science of linguistics, in which what we know is dwarfed by what we do not know but are fascinated to find out.

Yet this very revolution has presented many teachers with a new problem: whether they liked the old grammar or not, they do not understand the new approaches and find it rather difficult, with the best will in the world, to get hold of books that will explain them in terms sufficiently simple to communicate to pupils in the classroom.

This book is an attempt to explain modern grammatical knowledge in terms that can be generally understood, and even communicated to pupils. Such a task is not an easy one. Nearly all the important knowledge is available only in highly complex and rigidly academic books and articles. Any attempt to break down the degree of difficulty of the material, so that nonspecialists may find it readable, can succeed only at the expense of some accuracy and some completeness. The problem is how to arrive at the best compromise: how to obtain the maximum clarity with the least sacrifice of accuracy.

One of the dangers is that, in trying to explain the unfamiliar in terms of the familiar, one can easily give the impression that the unfamiliar is more like the familiar than it really is. But it is necessary to take this risk, unless we are to face the alternative of divorcing classroom information completely from present-day technical knowledge.

The rest of this chapter will be devoted to an account of the revolutionary change that has affected grammar in recent years.

1.2 THE ORIGINS OF TRADITIONAL GRAMMAR

When people want to check on one of the rules of English grammar, they go to a grammar book, and it would probably never occur to most people to question this authority. It is assumed that the authors are to be trusted, just as our teachers were trusted. But where do authors of grammar books get their facts from? The so-called facts of conventional grammar books (right down to the present time) were first codified in the eighteenth century and have been copied from one grammar book to another over a period of about two hundred years. (Not "copied" in any plagiaristic sense, but the ideas of one absorbed and passed on in the next.) Grammars had been written before the eighteenth century but generally with the aim of teaching English to foreigners or of providing a guide to Latin grammar. In general, it was not until the middle of the eighteenth century that the tradition began which gave rise to the modern conventional grammar book.

In coming to their decisions about grammar, those early writers were guided by two influences: logic and Latin grammar. Now, although it seemed to scholars of those days that problems of language could be solved by considering logic, scholars today would deny this. They would claim that language is meant to be expressive and sometimes defies logic in order to be colorful or emotional, or because the expression that is illogical is nevertheless clear to everyone. Let us take an example. In the eighteenth century, it was first decreed that words like *perfect, round*, and *square* could not be "compared"—that is, they could not have a comparative degree. If something is perfect, scholars said, it cannot be more perfect, since it has already reached a point beyond which it is impossible to go. Similarly, if something is round, it cannot be rounder. There is no doubt that this reasoning was logical, and if language were always logical, there would be nothing more to be said. But language is not always logical. If a teacher says to a child in a geometry lesson, *Try to make your circle rounder*, he is saying something that is logically absurd. If the figure is round, then it cannot be made rounder; if it is not, then the logical thing to say is *Make it round.* Indeed, we might go further and say that if the figure is a circle, it is already round, and so the teacher's remark is pointless. That is the strictly logical point of view. But we all know that if someone says, *Make that circle rounder* or *Come squarer to the wicket*, what is being said is not senseless but conveys a meaning that we well understand. Spoken language is very fast, and people have not time to be constantly checking what they say for logical errors. When they write, they are able to keep a somewhat closer check on logic; but, even then, there is no need for hesitation over the use of an illogical expression if it is meaningful and likely to be understood by all who read it. When you come to think of it, the fact that it is not logical hurts no one, since everyone understands that what is being said is not meant to be logically exact.

I hope no one will imagine that I am saying that logic has no place in language, or that we can forget all about it when we write. By no means. But I am saying that we need not be rigidly bound by it.

The other resort of eighteenth-century grammarians was Latin grammar. Decisions about the rules for English were sometimes arrived at through a transfer of the rules for Latin. That is why old-fashioned grammar books talk about accusative and dative cases, though these terms have no real application to English; about gender in nouns, though gender in English nouns is merely a part of their meaning; about rules asserting that the verb *to be* must take the same case after it as before, though this rule is not true for English.

We should not be scornful of their errors. The view of language taken in the eighteenth century was that there was a theoretical structure common to all languages; hence it was not *foolish* to apply the rules of Latin to English. And although it is clear today that the surface structure of all languages is not the same, it seems quite feasible that there is a universal underlying structure. It would seem reasonable to suggest, though, that statements about English grammar should be descriptions of what actually happens in English, not of what actually happens in Latin.

It begins to look less certain that the rules found in conventional grammar books are infallible or immutable when we see the poor justification that most of the rules had in the first place. Often, they were merely the whims of particular scholars (for example, the conventional rules for the use of *shall* and *will*). It cannot even be claimed that the scholars were always ones whose instinctive judgments we would respect.

1.3 MODERN ATTITUDES TOWARD CORRECTNESS

One modern writer, C. C. Fries, has referred to the grammar that I learned at school as belonging to a "prescientific era." His remark implies that grammar is now more scientific than it was. But what does this mean? It certainly does not mean that grammar is exactly the same sort of subject as physics, but it does mean that the theoretical basis of inquiry, which is often called scientific method, has in recent years been applied to grammar — with spectacular results. Indeed, the results have been even more spectacular since Fries wrote his comment.

An important result of the application of scientific method to grammar has been a change in aim. Whereas the older grammarians tried to lay down what sort of language *ought* to be used, the modern ones are more concerned with trying to describe what language *is* used. They do not forbid you to use *I will* as a simple future, since nearly everybody does so use it. Nor do they command that a sentence must not end with a preposition. Nor that every sentence must have a principal clause. (Look at that one, for instance.) Since people sometimes say *the council is* and sometimes *the council are*, modern grammarians approve of both.

But some people are not comfortable about this new approach. The easy tolerance disturbs them, and they often protest that it leads to the notion that anything is right. It doesn't, of course; all that it does lead to is the notion that more than one form may be acceptable. Correctness is considered to be a matter of conforming to the language fashions around you. If you do conform, people probably won't object to your way of speaking or writing; if you don't, they probably will. That is why, in a sense, you are your own best grammar book. Some people, no doubt, have a better ear for language than others, just as some have a better ear for music; and if a person cannot trust his ear in either, he has to accept the fact that he will never be a connoisseur. Other people cannot appreciate music for him, and, ultimately, they cannot make discriminations in language for him, because he has to speak so often that he is forced to rely on his own judgment. Still, instruction may draw his attention to the general patterns of the language as it is spoken and written in our community, and so help his own awareness of it.

This book does not prescribe any standards that ought to be imposed, nor does it attempt to make any contribution to the problems of improving oral or written expression. It presupposes that language will be taught as an interesting phenomenon in its own right.

1.4 SPOKEN AND WRITTEN ENGLISH

The old grammars concentrated heavily on written language. Sentences for exercises were often taken from literature, even from such sources as the Bible, in which the language was not contemporary. The result was that many sentences used in grammar books were such as would be unlikely to be used by the people who studied them, while the language used by these people was virtually ignored by the grammar books.

Modern language scholars have rebelled against the older emphasis on written language and have pointed out that the overwhelming majority of language used in the community is spoken. Many have argued from this that speech is the more important part of the language and that instruction should be based on the patterns of spoken English. Speech existed before writing, and writing developed mainly as a method of recording speech, so that in this sense speech can be considered primary. For a time, modern scholars concentrated almost exclusively on spoken language. It was important to redress the balance and renew people's awareness of the importance of speech, but it is now being realized that the pendulum swung back too far. The fact is that the community commits many of its most important statements to writing, so that there is a kind of importance possessed by some written language that is not usually possessed by speech. Surely the most sensible policy is to recognize that speech and writing each have an importance of a different sort and that mastery of the language involves mastery of both. An attempt has been made in this book to take into account both spoken and written forms.

1.5 DISSATISFACTION WITH TRADITIONAL PARTS OF SPEECH

One of the consequences of the adoption of a more scientific approach to grammar was that the old definitions of parts of speech were re-examined more critically than ever before. A couple of generations ago, such a thing would have been unthinkable, since nothing seemed more final and closed than the procedures of parsing and analysis. Grammar was not the kind of study where progress seemed either likely or necessary, since the existing procedures purported to explain everything that there was to be known about the structure of the language. But the new approach to language studies has shaken the very foundation of the system and has caused tremors to be felt in almost every wing and corridor.

Let us have a look at some of the older definitions of parts of speech. For a long time it was customary to say that a verb was a "doing, being, or having word"; yet by this definition we would expect the words *action*, *existence*, and *possession* to be verbs, rather than nouns, as they are traditionally said to be. And what about a word like *run*? Can it be a "doing word" in the sentence *I will run around the block* and yet cease to be one in the sentence *I will go for a run around the block*?

One of the older grammarians, J. C. Nesfield, defined a verb as "a word used for *saying* something about something else." It should be immediately obvious that this was not very satisfactory. Many kinds of words "say something about something else." In the phrase *a sick man, sick* says something about *man.* Now, I realize that this is not what Nesfield meant by "saying"; but it is difficult to know what he *did* mean. It is clear that a more precise definition of a verb must be sought.

Perhaps the trouble is that Nesfield's wording was too vague, and what he meant could be expressed more clearly. Here is a definition (taken from another conventional grammarian) which expresses more explicitly what I think Nesfield meant: "The verb is that part of speech by means of which we make an assertion or ask a question." This is better, perhaps, but statements can be made and questions asked without making use of any of the words conventionally described as verbs. After a walk to his front gate to look in the letter box, a man may report to his wife, *Nothing today*, and she may ask, *Nothing at all?* A statement has been made and a question asked, but no verbs have been used at all. The conventional answer to this is that there is a verb "understood." But which verb is understood? *Nothing today* may be expanded into *There is nothing today, Nothing has come today, Nothing has been left today, I found nothing in the box today, The postman delivered nothing today, The postman brought nothing today*, and goodness knows how many other sentences. Likewise, the question *Nothing at all?* may be expanded into questions which correspond to the statements just listed. Now, it is true that in all of these a general idea is understood, but it is not at all clear which particular *verb* is understood or how we could decide which one is.

Now let us look at nouns. The conventional definition tells us that a noun is "a word used for naming anything," and it usually adds that "anything" includes person, place, quality, action, feeling, collection, etc. The difficulty is that many words that are not considered nouns could be described by this definition. In the sentence *My book is red*, it could surely be argued that *red* is the name of a quality. In *The meeting will be here*, the word *here* names a place. If we say *You mustn't walk; what you must do is skip*, the word *skip* names the action.

Nouns have not been clearly separated from adjectives in conventional grammar. In *the school concert, school* fulfills the function of an adjective, in that it "describes" or "adds to the meaning of" *concert*, yet it also has some of the qualities of a noun, as can be seen from the variation *combined schools concert*, where the noun ending *-s* is added to this word. There is the further difficulty of how to classify *poor* in *The poor are deserving of help.*

There is not space here to describe all the arguments against conventional definitions of parts of speech, but I have indicated the sorts of objections that are raised against almost every conventional definition. The trouble is that conventional grammar has tried to put words into classes according to two different criteria. Sometimes the classes are based on meaning ("a verb is a doing, being, or having word"), and sometimes they are based on function ("an adjective is a word that qualifies a noun"). Now, if you are going to classify anything, you should deal with only one criterion at a time. Let us suppose that you have a lot of books, all English literature, which you want to arrange on your shelves according to some well-organized plan. You can, if you wish, make your main groupings according to the type of literature in each book; that is, you may put all your novels together in one group, plays in another, poetry books in another, and so on. Then, if you wish, you can arrange the books within any one group according to the period when they were written. Within the main group "Poetry," there would be subsections "Sixteenth Century," "Seventeenth Century," etc. Your procedure will be perfectly sound; but it would not have been, if you had mixed the two criteria at the same level. It would have been a mistake to have made your first main category "Poetry," and your second one "Sixteenth-Century Literature." There would be some books that would belong to two groups at once, and you would not know how to classify them. Well, something like this mistake has been made in the traditional attempts to classify words: the criteria of meaning and function have become mixed. There are words that fit the definition of nouns according to their meaning, and of adjectives according to their function, and so on.

It is quite possible that you may think of some objections to some of the points I have been making. You may feel that you could patch up the old definitions by changing the wording a little. The truth is, however, that many scholars have spent a great deal of time trying to arrive at watertight definitions for the parts of speech by conventional methods, and all have failed. If you feel you can succeed, by all means try.

1.6 NEW METHODS OF CLASSIFICATION

The old definitions leaned heavily on meaning, though, as we have seen, some of them were based on function. As a matter of fact, even their function often meant "what part their meaning played in the semantic complex of the sentence." The modern grammarians for a time excluded consideration of meaning from their operations, feeling that science could not study such a phenomenon. Today, linguists are coming around to the view that it is not unscientific to study mentalistic phenomena such as meaning (see 2.3, 11.2), but it is unlikely that there will be a return to the sort of use of it that was made in conventional grammar. In any case, grammarians in the immediate past have concentrated on other criteria, especially the positions that words could occupy in sentence structure. The change in emphasis has led to a great many interesting discoveries, and has caused renewed interest in a subject that had previously stagnated for a long time. The next chapter will provide a brief survey of several of the modern attempts to find a more satisfactory grammar than the traditional one.

2
STRUCTURAL AND
TRANSFORMATIONAL GRAMMAR

2.1 *THE STRUCTURE OF ENGLISH*

In 1952, *The Structure of English* by C. C. Fries was
published in America, and it has had a considerable
influence since on the teaching of English throughout
the world. Fries was only one of many scholars who
arrived at much the same sort of theoretical position
at about the same time. While his book is less rigidly
academic than some others covering similar territory
(such as *Methods in Structural Linguistics* by Zellig
Harris, 1951), this very fact has made its contents
more accessible to teachers. Besides, Fries's approach
has been popularly developed by such writers as Paul
Roberts, and this has helped it to be even more available to those who are interested in it.

There is an inevitable delay between the publication
of an idea and its application in the classroom, and so,
ironically, a knowledge of Fries's work began to spread
among teachers at about the same time as it was be-
coming obsolete. No linguistic scholar today would seriously claim that *The Structure of English* was the
best account, or even an adequate one, of the grammar

14

of English. Yet it was a very important work, and many of the lessons it carries are still worth learning.

Since Fries regarded conventional grammar as belonging to a "prescientific era," he was anxious to replace it by a grammar worked out by scientific means. It was his intention to start right from the beginning, almost as if conventional grammar did not exist, and try to build up a grammar by extracting the natural structure of the language.

He tried to put out of his mind the notions he had learned from conventional grammar, and to this end he decided not to use the conventional names for parts of speech. Any word classes that he discovered were to be labeled by numbers and letters. He tried to approach his task without preconceptions, evolving a description of the language solely from observing it.

He was committed to the view that spoken language was primary, and so he decided to collect samples of it as it was heard in the community around him. His whole aim was to *describe* the language, and not at all to *prescribe* what people ought to say. To this end, he tape-recorded about fifty hours of ordinary telephone conversations, conducted by people who did not know they were being recorded.

Fries planned to allot words to the same part of speech if they could fill the same set of positions in English sentences. This was a completely different basis for classification from the conventional one, which comprised meaning and function.

In order to find out which words could occur in which positions, he took test sentences and tried substituting other words in each of the positions. For instance, he took *The concert was good* and tried to find out which words could be substituted for *concert* without changing the structure of the sentence. He submitted each substitution to the judgment of native speakers of English, with the request that they tell him whether it was structurally "the same as" or "different from" the original sentence. The words which were described as leaving the structure the same, he grouped together as class 1: words like *food, coffee, taste, container.* By using this technique in different positions, Fries isolated four main parts of speech or FORM CLASSES† which he numbered 1, 2, 3, and 4. In order to convey some concept of these classes in a very short space, we may say that they are rather similar to the conventional categories, nouns, verbs, adjectives, and adverbs, though Fries rightly warned his readers against equating his classes with the conventional ones. They are somewhat different in content, and very different in conception, but we may make a rough equation here. In addition, Fries found fifteen groups of other words, which he called FUNCTION WORDS and labeled A to O. These were words which operated mainly to convey signals of structure. There was an important difference between the concept of form classes and that of function groups. The four form classes each contain thousands of items, and new items are constantly added. Because of this, they are technically called OPEN classes. The function groups on the other hand are CLOSED, that is, they have a limited number of members, and new items are hardly ever added. Fries claimed that there were only 154 words altogether in his fifteen function groups.

†Technical terms appearing in small capitals are to be found in the glossary at the back of this book.

When you consider that conventional grammar usually describes about eight WORD CLASSES, as compared with Fries's nineteen, you can see that his results were quite different from the traditional ones. Others have tried other approaches and obtained slightly different results, but on the whole there is fair agreement among different studies of grammar by structural methods.

2.2 WORD CLASSES BY SUBSTITUTION

The process of SUBSTITUTION employed by Fries has been used by practically all modern investigators, and is still of considerable importance in any grammatical description. Many people, like Fries, have tried to show that a sentence consists of a sequence of words, each of which represents a whole class. The idea may be illustrated fairly simply. Let us consider a sentence such as *These rather beautiful designs won.* Each of the words in this sequence could be exchanged for a number of other words, as shown in the accompanying diagram.

THESE	RATHER	BEAUTIFUL	DESIGNS	WON
THE	FAIRLY	OLD	FILMS	FADED
THOSE	EXTREMELY	POPULAR	BOOKS	DETERIORATED
MY	VERY	FANCY	COSTUME	SUCCEEDED
HIS	QUITE	IMPRESSIVE	PORTRAITS	FAILED

The words that can replace *these* would be grouped with it to form a class, those that can replace *rather* would be grouped to form another class, and so on throughout the five substitutions. It is often true that the group of words that can replace each other in one position will also be interchangeable in other positions in English sentences, and so a word class of this kind is a group of words that can fill the same set of positions as each other. Grammars of this kind have been popular until fairly recently, and it must be conceded that they produce results that are fairly workable for the classroom. On the whole, grammarians who have followed this "structural" type of grammar have abandoned Fries's scrupulous avoidance of the conventional names of the parts of speech and have taken the view that it is better to use names that are familiar, even if the concepts are somewhat changed. So, the term "noun" is frequently still used; but a word is a noun, not because it is the name of something, but because it is capable of filling a certain set of positions in the sentence-patterns of English. Most structural grammarians, while keeping the conventional names, have also had to invent more, since they nearly always have more classes than the conventional eight.

It so happens that any word in the diagram can combine with any set of representatives of the other four classes, but that is only because these examples have been carefully chosen, and it is not a necessary condition of classification. We now proceed to a fuller discussion of this problem.

2.3 GRAMMAR AND SEMANTICS

Linguists make a distinction between a grammatically well-formed sentence and one that is also semantically satisfactory, that is, makes sense. Let us look at an example that will make this clear. Everyone would agree that the following is not a satisfactory English sentence:

> Egg accurate luxuriously park aggressive the
> thwarted the

One of the reasons is that it is not grammatically well-formed. We know that the order of the word classes is not an English one. If we try substituting other words of the same grammatical classes for the ones just given, we will never arrive at a meaningful sentence. Now let us rearrange the order of the words:

> The aggressive egg luxuriously thwarted the
> accurate park

This is still not a satisfactory English sentence, but any native speaker of the language will be aware that it seems somehow closer to the mark than the previous sequence. The explanation is that there is now nothing strange about the order of the word classes: this sentence follows the grammatical pattern of an English statement. The only trouble is the sequence doesn't make sense. We would say, then, that this sentence is grammatically well-formed, though it is not semantically satisfactory. We could make it completely acceptable by substituting other words of the same grammatical categories, such as *The black dog furiously attacked the timid cat.*

When we say that there is a sentence-pattern for English consisting of, say, NOUN + VERB, we do not mean that any noun can be coupled with any verb to make a sentence, but rather that every noun can be coupled with some verbs, and every verb with some nouns. This principle applies throughout the whole range of grammatical patterns.

2.4 IMMEDIATE CONSTITUENTS

Sense is conveyed not only by the dictionary meanings of words but also by their arrangement in patterns. A sentence is not just a linear string of words; it is a sequence grouped in a particular way. The groupings are important for understanding the sense, and a great many ambiguous sentences are not clear because the groupings are not clear. For instance, consider the phrase *an old lecturer's gown*. Without further information, we cannot be sure whether this phrase refers to *the gown of an old lecturer* or *the old gown of a lecturer*. For each of these meanings, the words are grouped in a different way. If the meaning is *the gown of an old lecturer*, the groupings can be shown thus:

an old lecturer's / gown

On the other hand, if the meaning is *the old gown of a lecturer*, the groupings would be better shown thus:

an old / lecturer's gown

To take another example, the sentence *The bowling greens are available for ladies only on Tuesdays and Thursdays* is ambiguous, as can be seen from the following pair of groupings:

The bowling greens are available for ladies only /
on Tuesdays and Thursdays
The bowling greens are available for ladies /
only on Tuesdays and Thursdays

The groupings of words in a sentence are referred to as its CONSTITUENTS. Generally there is a whole hierarchy of groupings. Let us now take an example of an extremely simple sentence and gradually and continuously multiply the constituents.

One of the simplest sentences that it is possible to have in English is a two-word sequence such as:

AUSTRALIANS	TRAVEL

We say that this sentence is made up of two CONSTITU-ENTS, *Australians* and *travel*. Now, if we wanted to, we could substitute a two-word sequence for the constituent *Australians*, without changing the basic structure—let us say, *people abroad*. The best way of illustrating what we have done would be this:

AUSTRALIANS		TRAVEL
PEOPLE	ABROAD	

The sentence still has two main constituents: *people abroad* and *travel*, but now the first of these main constituents consists of two smaller ones. It is customary to call the main parts of any structure its IMMEDIATE CONSTITUENTS, while any smaller part is a CONSTITU-ENT. Thus, the immediate constituents of the first sentence above are *Australians* and *travel*, and it has no smaller constituents. The immediate constituents of the second sentence are *people abroad* and *travel*. The single word *people* is a constituent, but not an immediate constituent of the phrase *people abroad*.

Now, let us substitute for *travel* an item made up of two smaller constituents. The situation may be represented thus:

AUSTRALIANS		TRAVEL	
PEOPLE	ABROAD	SHIFT	CONSTANTLY

If we want to carry this process on further, we can expand each of these four constituents into a sequence of two smaller constituents. Suppose that for *people* I substitute *my friends;* for *abroad, in Europe;* for *shift, move about;* and for *constantly, every day.* The result will be as follows:

AUSTRALIANS			TRAVEL			
PEOPLE		ABROAD	SHIFT		CONSTANTLY	
MY	FRIENDS	IN EUROPE	MOVE	ABOUT	EVERY	DAY

Finally, if we wished, we could expand some constituents but not others. For *friends,* let us write *wealthy friends;* for *Europe, the Riviera;* and for *move, are moving.*

AUSTRALIANS				TRAVEL				
PEOPLE			ABROAD	SHIFT			CONSTANTLY	
MY	FRIENDS		IN	EUROPE	MOVE		ABOUT	EVERY	DAY
MY	WEALTHY	FRIENDS	ON	THE RIVIERA	ARE	MOVING	ABOUT	EVERY	DAY

This is by no means the extent of the expansions that are theoretically possible; but let us pause now and abstract from the preceding a representation of the constituent structure of the final sentence:

MY WEALTHY FRIENDS ON THE RIVIERA ARE MOVING ABOUT EVERY DAY

The system followed here is that pairs of immediate constituents are marked off by right-angled brackets placed back-to-back, thus:

At the bottom of the diagram stands the largest pair of brackets, showing that the immediate constituents of the whole sentence are: *my wealthy friends on the Riviera* and *are moving about every day*. If we look at the first of these and raise our eyes one line higher, we can see that the immediate constituents of *my wealthy friends on the Riviera* are *my wealthy friends* and *on the Riviera*. *My wealthy friends* then divides into *my* and *wealthy friends*, and the latter phrase into *wealthy* and *friends*. Other components of the sentence can be traced in the same way.

Because every word is ultimately divided off from every other word, the reader may be misled into thinking that every sequence of words is a constituent of something; but this is not so. *The Riviera are* is not a constituent of anything, nor is *moving about every*. The constituent groupings are made in a way that reflects our intuitive knowledge about the construction of the sentence.

2.5 CONSTITUENT STRUCTURE GRAMMAR

Fries and others who have tried to work out a grammar based on positions have always been careful to take account of CONSTITUENT STRUCTURE. The reason is that constituents are manifestations of patterning, and patterning introduces order where there would otherwise be chaos.

Let us consider again the sentence that was expanded in the last section:

AUSTRALIANS TRAVEL

Previously, both constituents were expanded, but it will simplify the description here if we first expand only the initial immediate constituent, and leave *travel* as a constant second part of each sentence. We will use the same expansions of the first component as before, to produce these sentences:

AUSTRALIANS	TRAVEL
PEOPLE ABROAD	
MY FRIENDS IN EUROPE	
MY WEALTHY FRIENDS ON THE RIVIERA	

Each of the items on the left-hand side, as we have seen, performs the same role in the structure of the sentence as the others do. This is a very important fact, for it means that we can describe the structure of each of the preceding sentences by the same general formula. Suppose we use the term NOUN PHRASE to label each of the items on the left-hand side. We can then say that each sentence consists of the pattern:

NOUN PHRASE + VERB

But similar facts can be shown for the expansions of *travel*:

AUSTRALIANS	TRAVEL
	SHIFT CONSTANTLY
	MOVE ABOUT EVERY DAY
	ARE MOVING ABOUT EVERY DAY

We may refer to the four items on the right-hand side as PREDICATE PHRASES, for we have already seen that they are equivalent constituents in the structure of the sentence. But we now see that the common formula:

NOUN PHRASE + PREDICATE PHRASE

applies to each of the sentences formed by combining one of these predicate phrases with one of the noun phrases.

Each constituent involved in a structure (except the very smallest and the very largest) has two aspects: an internal one and an external one. The noun phrases listed earlier all have different internal structures and must be analyzed differently; but in relation to larger structures than themselves they are equivalent items. All the predicate phrases are also equivalent constituents that have differing internal structures.

These facts simplify the total description of sentences. We can first describe the positions of the various classes of words within, say, a noun phrase, and then describe the numerous positions in which noun phrases can occur. This eliminates a great deal of repetition. Having described the internal structure of noun phrases once, we can thereafter concern ourselves exclusively with their external roles and treat all of them as units.

The internal analysis of a noun phrase (or any other structure) can be made in terms of constituents. The noun phrase *my wealthy friends on the Riviera* can be described as consisting of a smaller noun phrase, *my wealthy friends*, and a prepositional phrase, *on the Riviera.* This prepositional phrase can then be said to consist of a preposition, *on*, and a smaller noun phrase, *the Riviera.* Finally, this noun phrase can be said to consist of representatives of two word classes: a determiner and a noun.

2.6 CONVENTIONAL GRAMMAR AND CONSTITUENT STRUCTURE

Although the classification of words in conventional grammar was not made on the basis of positions, there was usually some description of constituents: sentences were cut into clauses, clauses into subjects and predicates, each of these into phrases, and so on. Or, working the other way, illustrations were given to show how a single word could be replaced by a phrase or a clause, for example,

A *huge* man appeared in the doorway

A man *of huge stature* appeared in the doorway

A man *who was huge* appeared in the doorway

The adjective, adjectival phrase, and adjectival clause italicized here would be equated by a conventional description. Similar equations would be made for adverbs, adverbial phrases, and adverbial clauses, and for nouns, noun phrases, and noun clauses.

In broad details, conventional grammar could be described as a type of constituent structure grammar. Structural grammarians such as Fries paid much more attention to constituent structure and were much more systematic in their study of it, but they did not invent it.

2.7 TRANSFORMATIONAL GRAMMAR

Until a few years ago, linguists thought it might be possible to describe the whole of English sentence structure by a system of immediate constituents. All sorts of methods were developed in order to provide a satisfactory constituent analysis, and gradually two facts emerged. The first was that, as far as they went, many of these methods were effective; and, indeed, many of them were simply variations on the same basic method. The second was that the task of describing English or any other language completely in terms of immediate constituents was very difficult indeed. Finally, in 1957, in a book called *Syntactic Structures*, the American linguist Noam Chomsky proved to the satisfaction of most linguists that it could not be done. He did not reject the whole notion of using immediate constituents; he merely showed that this method was not powerful enough by itself to account for the whole of sentence structure. It must be used in conjunction with some other method.

The other method developed by Chomsky has now become widely known as TRANSFORMATIONAL GRAMMAR. It was first expounded in *Syntactic Structures*, and has been revised and somewhat changed in Chomsky's *Aspects of the Theory of Syntax* (1965). The following explanation of transformational grammar is based on these two books but is greatly simplified (and, to that extent, distorted) for the present purposes of explication. Certain sentences of English, called KERNEL SENTENCES, have the simplest structures, and more complex sentences are derived either from one of them or from a sequence of them. The kernels are such that they could be adequately described, or very nearly so, by constituent structure methods, and the more complex sentences, which could not, are derived from them by the application of transformational rules. Strictly, we should say that the complex sentences are derived from the structures underlying the kernel sentences, rather than the kernel sentences themselves, but we will often disregard this difference here. We might explain the role of kernels by drawing an analogy with a musical work, in which the total design is made up of a number of simpler themes, each of which has a structure of its own.

The major part of this book will be devoted to describing the structure of English in terms of the insights provided by transformational grammar. There will first be a description, in terms of constituent structure, of the kernel sentences of English; then it will be shown how other structures are effected by changes (transformations) wrought on the basic structures of kernel sentences.

Chomsky caused a tremendous change in the aims of grammarians. Previously, they had attempted to provide only an analysis of sentence structure. They took sentences of English (recorded from the conversations of native speakers of the language) and tried to devise scientific procedures for analyzing the sentences into their component parts. Technically, what they were often trying to do was devise a DISCOVERY PROCEDURE; they wanted to find out not only what the structure of English was but also how this structure could be discovered, step by step, from the raw material, the spoken sentences of the language. Chomsky pointed out that no other science had achieved, or expected to achieve, a discovery procedure, and that linguists were undertaking an impossible task. It was as if, not content with being shown that Newton's theory of gravitation accounted for a lot of facts, we demanded a step-by-step description of how he arrived at it. Chomsky suggested that instead of worrying about how a description of language could be arrived at, we ought to accept any description that seemed to fit the facts, no matter how it was obtained.

Chomsky's grammar is not only transformational but also GENERATIVE. That means it consists of a set of rules for generating the sentences of the language. The rules can be arrived at by any means at all, including intuition; but, having been enunciated, they must then be tested for validity. That is, the sentences generated by the rules must be compared with the actual sentences of the language. Chomsky tried, success-fully, to create rules which would enumerate an infinite number of sentences. Of course, a natural language like English changes from day to day, and it does not seem feasible that a grammar could ever predict ex-actly the sentences it contains. We must be satisfied to hope for a high degree of correlation.

Chomsky is interested in doing more than just gener-ating the sentences of the language. In the process of generating them, he wants to provide certain infor-mation about their structure and show how different structures are related to each other. Transformational grammar can do this in ways that are impossible for a grammar that consists only of constituent structure rules.

At present, the aim of achieving a complete transfor-mational grammar of English or any other language seems far from fulfillment. We are not able to provide a grammar that will produce "all and only" the sen-tences of English. Nevertheless, so much fruitful re-search has been done since 1957 that it is now possi-ble to give a useful description of English using the new methods. I believe that such a grammar provides greater insight into English, and is more interesting, than conventional grammar. Teachers and students must give up the expectation that a grammar book will provide them with a ready-made and complete descrip-tion of English, and must rather try to follow with in-terest the partial knowledge that has been acquired by the science of linguistics.

If you have been brought up on conventional gram-mar, all of this may seem extremely unsatisfactory. After all, conventional grammar books were usually designed to give all the answers; there did not seem to be huge areas of the work which the grammarian could not explain, and what is being put forward here may seem incomplete and may even seem to raise more questions than it answers. Now, conventional grammar never did give all the answers; it simply ignored a lot of questions, and it is true that modern grammar is not as complete as conventional grammar *claimed* it was. Indeed, the science of linguistics, including that part of it which is concerned with grammar, is only in its infancy. Any grammarian today who pretended that there were not large areas of his subject where knowledge was lacking would be a charlatan. It perhaps requires a difficult adjustment of attitude to be satisfied with this state of affairs after thinking of grammar as a closed story, where all the facts were known. The compensation is that the whole subject has become much more interesting and vital than it was a generation ago.

As a matter of fact, the gulf between conventional grammar and modern generative grammar is not as great as may at first appear. Chomsky himself has pointed out that his form of grammar is closer to conventional grammar than many others are, and it is certainly true that he unhesitatingly draws on the insights provided by conventional grammar.

3
KERNEL STRUCTURES
IN ENGLISH

In order to understand the structure of the most complicated English sentence-patterns, we have to begin by studying the simplest. These are called the KERNEL-PATTERNS of the language, as we have seen, and even the most complicated sentences are elaborations of the structure of the kernels.

The simplest kernel-type in English consists of just two words, such as *Australians travel*. As everyone knows, the first word is a noun, and the second one a verb. Indeed, that is a sufficient working definition for both word classes for the moment: a noun is the word that occurs first in two-word manifestations of the basic English sentence-pattern, and a verb is the word that occurs second. They will be described in fuller detail later, but for the present that will do.

We saw in the last chapter that these two words, which are the immediate constituents of the simple sentence *Australians travel*, can be replaced by longer sequences. Each of the sequences that replaces *Australians* will play the same structural role as that sin-

31

gle word does, and for that reason the sequences are usually called NOUN PHRASES. In like manner, all the sequences that can replace *travel*, while keeping the same structural relationship to the noun phrase, are called PREDICATE PHRASES. The basic English sentence-pattern illustrated by *Australians travel* can therefore be said to consist of the sequence NOUN PHRASE + PREDICATE PHRASE:

AUSTRALIANS	TRAVEL
NOUN PHRASE	PRED PHRASE

Noun phrases in this position are often called subjects, and the same varieties can occur in all of the kernel-patterns to be described for English. In other words, the differences between the individual kernel-patterns occur in the predicate phrases. It will be useful to describe a standard type of noun phrase that occurs in English, before presenting the kernel-patterns.

3.2 THE NOUN PHRASE IN KERNEL SENTENCES

The standard pattern for the noun phase of a kernel sentence is:

(DETERMINER) + NOMINAL WORD

This is expressed in such a way as to allow for several variations. The reader may not yet know what a determiner is, but he can see that it is enclosed in parentheses, a sign that it may or may not occur. Indeed, there are some nominal words with which determiners never occur.

This simple formulation covers the occurrence of diverse noun phrases, including the following:

men	some friends	an apple
the men	anybody	he
a boy	something	we

We now proceed to a description of the categories involved.

3.3 DETERMINERS

DETERMINER is one of the class names that have been adopted in modern grammars, as additions to the conventional names. The class includes the following words when they occur in the same structural role as *the* in a noun phrase:

a	these	much	every	few
an	those	many	neither	less
the	some	each	either	several
this	any	no	enough	all
that	most	another	more	both

Several groups within the class are often given distinguishing labels: *a, an,* and *the* are referred to as articles; *this, that, these,* and *those* as demonstratives; and the rest as quantifiers.

Some of the determiners, namely, *these, those, many, most, few, several, all* (except when it occurs before another determiner), and *both,* are typically used with plural nominals, while *a, an, this, that, each, another, much, every, neither,* and *either* are used only with singulars. There is also a distinction between *a* and *an,* namely, that *a* is used only when the next word begins with a consonant sound, while *an* is used only when the next word begins with a vowel sound or diphthong.

All and *both* differ from the others in that they can precede other determiners. For this reason, we may refer to them as SPECIAL DETERMINERS. There is another way in which they differ from the other determiners: they can occur at the end of a noun phrase, instead of the beginning. Thus, we can say either *All the boys* (*go*) or *The boys all* (*go*).

Possessive forms such as *John's, my, ladies'* are very much like determiners in many respects. However, it is better not to include them here but to derive them by transformation from their equivalent nouns and pronouns. This will be done at a later point.

3.4 NOUNS

The term NOMINAL WORD embraces two kinds of words, nouns and pronouns. Though they act similarly in many ways, it will be convenient to discuss them separately.

It is customary to refer to certain nouns as proper nouns. In writing, they are easy to become familiar with, because they are spelled with a capital letter in all circumstances. In speech there are no capital letters, but we still have a knowledge of the items that are proper nouns (perhaps partly from our knowledge of the written conventions). They include Christian names, surnames, place names, names of rivers, mountains, etc., names of countries, days of the week, months of the year, titles of books, films, etc., brand names, names of institutions, etc. Nouns that are not proper nouns are said to be common nouns.

Conventional grammar also distinguishes between abstract and concrete nouns, the first category including words like *pain, love, hatred,* and *innocence,* and the second including ones like *book, car, fence,* and *tree.* There are grave difficulties about defining the two groups in any mutually exclusive way, but the difficulties concern mainly the boundary between the categories, and it is useful to be able to talk about abstract and common nouns. Indeed, the categories have been used in modern syntactic theory and in generative semantic theory.

The most important attribute of nouns is their number, either singular or plural. This matter will be discussed in detail shortly.

3.5 PRONOUNS

The main difference between nouns and pronouns is that pronouns are almost never accompanied by determiners. There are several groups of them:

Personal Pronouns

Unlike nouns, personal pronouns are differentiated according to their person. First person is the label applied to pronouns that refer to the speaker(s) or to the writer(s), second person to those which refer to the person(s) being addressed, and third person to those which refer to other people or things. The plural pronoun of the first person, *we*, conforms to this description only loosely. It usually refers not to a plurality of speakers but to a group that includes the speaker and may also include those spoken to or those spoken about. In the third person singular (only) there is a differentiation made on the basis of gender, which in English is equivalent to sex. The personal pronouns that can occur in the subject of a kernel sentence are as follows:

	Sing	*Plur*
1*st*	I	we
2*nd*	you	you
3*rd*	he, she, it	they

Indefinite Pronouns

This is the label given to the words *nobody, anybody, everybody, somebody, no one, anyone, everyone, someone, nothing, anything, everything, something.* Like personal pronouns, they are rarely accompanied by determiners. (Occasionally aberrant forms occur, such as *That someone you dream about.*)

3.6 KERNEL-PATTERN 1

We have already seen that the kernel-patterns consist of two immediate constituents, the noun phrase and the predicate phrase. We have looked at the constitution of the noun phrase and noted that each of the varieties can go with any kind of predicate phrase.

An attempt will now be made to present a group of simple structures as kernel sentences of English. It must be stressed that this is neither a definitive listing nor even a universally approved one. The aim is to present, not *the* set of kernel-patterns, but *a* set; to acquaint the reader with a general approach to grammar, rather than to provide definitive details. (The latter would be an impossible goal.)

The first kernel-pattern is illustrated by the following sentence:

The baby probably will be like me

It would be possible to represent this sentence as a string of elements in this fashion:

DET	NOUN	PVB	AUX	BE	LIKE	NOUN
The	baby	probably	will	be	like	me

But we have already seen (2.4) that a simple string of WORD CLASSES does not give us enough information about the structure of a sentence. Both interpretations of the phrase *an old lecturer's gown* could be described by this string:

DET	ADJ	NOUN (POSS)	NOUN

If we want to differentiate between the two meanings, we have to show, in some such way as the following, how the items are grouped to make the two different structures.

An	old	lecturer's	gown
DET	ADJ	NOUN (POSS)	NOUN
QUALIFIER		NOMINAL GROUP	

An	old	lecturer's	gown
DET	ADJ	NOUN (POSS)	NOUN
QUALIFIER			NOMINAL GROUP

It is true that, with the sentence *The baby probably will be like me*, there seems little danger of ambiguity; nevertheless, if we try to show the structure by a simple string of elements, we will fail to present all the information necessary for describing it. And structural ambiguity *is* possible, even with this sentence. Imagine a discussion in which one person raises the question of whether the baby (when it is born) will be fair, and the other person replies, "The baby probably will be, like me." The same sequence of elements has been used as in the sentence quoted earlier, but the two are structurally different, and this must be shown in any description of the sentence patterns.

There are at least two convenient ways of showing the structure of a sentence such as *The baby probably will be like me.* One is to use a diagram containing boxes, like the ones used earlier for *an old lecturer's gown.* Another is to use what is called a branching tree diagram, like the one shown in Figure 3.1.

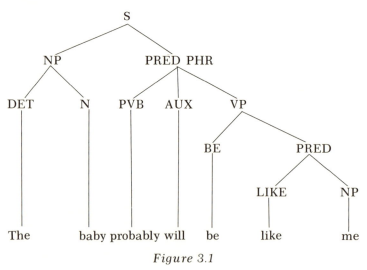

Figure 3.1

The following remarks must be made about this diagram:

1. "S" stands for "sentence," and the lines branching out from it eventually encompass the whole sentence. The labels at the end of these two lines show that the immediate constituents of this sentence are NP and PRED PHR.

2. "NP" is a standard abbreviation for "noun

phrase." In the diagram, it branches into two constituents: DET (determiner) and N (noun).

3. "PRED PHR" stands for "predicate phrase." It branches into three immediate constituents: PVB, AUX, and VP.

4. "PVB" stands for "preverb" or "preverbal adverbial," and there are two kinds:

POSITIVE: always, usually, frequently, often, probably, fortunately, certainly, etc.

NEGATIVE: never, scarcely, hardly, rarely, seldom, barely, little, etc.

5. In this and other kernel-patterns, there are three kinds of AUXILIARIES we must concern ourselves with:

a. MODAL AUXILIARIES: will, shall, would, could, should, can, may, might, must.

b. "HAVE," and its parts: have, has, had.

c. "BE" and its parts: be, been, being, am, is, are, was, were.

The entries under b are regarded by native speakers of English as being forms of the same word, and so are the entries under c; thus we can refer to the two groups as HAVE and BE for brevity.

The sentence component described as AUX (auxiliary) may consist of, not just one word, but a sequence, and the pattern for it is set by the formula:

$$(MODAL) + (HAVE) + (BE)$$

But the details of formation of auxiliaries are complex, and a description of them will be deferred until after all the kernel-patterns have been described.

6. There is a tendency for the preverb to move close to the main verb, and so we often find it moving to the other side of part or all of the auxiliary. *Max always will be a failure*, while a possible English sentence, is somewhat less likely than *Max will always be a failure.*

7. The word *be* in the diagram is intended to be a main verb, not part of the auxiliary. Once again, the symbol BE is intended to stand for any form of the word. The same forms can occur also as part of the auxiliary, even when the main verb is BE:

He *is being* on his best behavior

The word *is* here is an auxiliary, while *being* is a part of the main verb.

8. In the predicate phrase, special pronoun forms are sometimes found as realizations of the noun phrase: *me, him, her, us, them.*

9. This kernel-pattern, and all those to be described, can additionally have a place adverbial or a time adverbial, or both, attached to the predicate phrase. They may be either single-word adverbs, such as *here*, or phrases such as *in my office, in the afternoon.* They have been omitted from the diagrams for the sake of simplicity, and because they have a loose attachment to all the patterns, but it should be remembered that they can always occur.

Other examples of sentences following Pattern 1 are as follows:

I will soon be an uncle

He has been chairman in the past

The manager was like a beast at the meeting on Friday

3.7 KERNEL-PATTERN 2

The second pattern is similar to the first, except that the constituent PRED is manifested as an ADJECTIVE. Adjectives in a VP construction with BE are often called PREDICATIVE ADJECTIVES.

As an example of Kernel-Pattern 2, we will take the sentence *The men certainly should be tired.* It is illustrated in Figure 3.2.

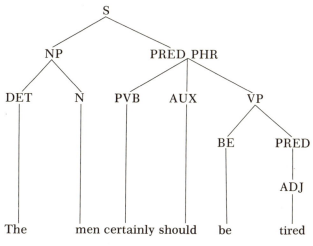

Figure 3.2

Wherever single-word adjectives can occur, so too can ADJECTIVAL CONSTRUCTS. This term refers to combinations consisting of:

INTENSIFIER +ADJECTIVE

The category INTENSIFIER includes such words as *very, rather, quite, really, particularly, extremely, fairly, exceedingly.*

3.8   KERNEL-PATTERN 3

One of the most difficult tasks in grammar is the systematic analysis of verbs, and it is a task that has not yet been completed by linguists, since there seems to be almost no limit to the complexities. Nevertheless, enough is known to provide a reasonably coherent description.

Having seen the patterns involving the verb BE, we must now turn to those involving TRANSITIVE VERBS, that is, those that may be followed by objects (noun phrases of just the same kinds as we have already examined). Here are some typical ones:

acknowledge	complete	please	surprise
admire	discover	remember	terrify
announce	eat	say	thank
astonish	find	see	understand
believe	hammer	smoke	write

Pattern 3 may be represented by the sentence *I can usually charge a book to my account.* This pattern is shown in Figure 3.3.

"PP" (prepositional phrase) consists of a preposition plus a noun phrase, such as *to my account.* Earlier, we saw that any of the kernel-patterns could be followed by place or time adverbials, and some of these adverbials are also prepositional phrases. But a distinction must be made between the place and time adverbials, which are loosely attached to the whole sentence, and this item PP, which has tight structural bonds with the verb. Though they may, on occasion, have an accidental similarity of appearance, the two lines are quite different in their relationships with the structure of the

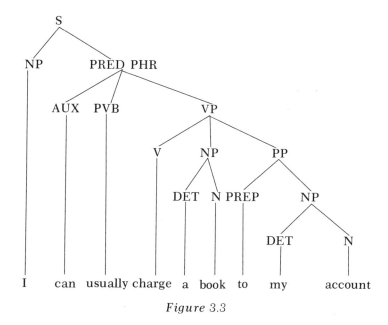

Figure 3.3

sentence. The difference may be seen in these sentences:

I charged the book *to my account*
(PP an integral part of Pattern 3)
I charged the book *on my way out*
(Adverbial loosely attached to the sentence)

A similar phenomenon may be observed when there is no object:

I drove into the garage
I drove in the afternoon

The item PP may involve a sequence of prepositional phrases, each an integral part of the pattern:

He spoke to the manager about his problem
Sometimes Pattern 3 can have an additional item in

the VP: a manner adverbial. It can follow only some transitive verbs, not all of them. Thus, we can have *The chairman performed his duties in a perfunctory way*, but we cannot add a manner adverbial to sentences like *The program included two solos*. The distinction between verbs that freely take manner adverbials and those that do not is an important one.

3.9   KERNEL-PATTERN 4

Sometimes a transitive verb will have a word following which is intimately related to it, and which combines with the verb to form a large syntactic unit, for example,

I *washed up* the dishes
The publishers *brought out* another edition
The secretary *took over* the organization
The children *put away* their books

The construction should not be confused with that of VERB + PP, which it superficially resembles. In Pattern 4, words like *up*, *out*, *over*, and *away* are called PARTICLES, and the combination of verb and particle is sometimes called a PHRASAL VERB. It is a fairly modern development in English. Often the combination has a different meaning from that of the verb by itself; for instance, *take over* has a different meaning from *take*. Not all transitive verbs participate in such constructions; in fact, the number of verbs that do is relatively small; but hundreds of different combinations are in frequent use. Pattern 4 is illustrated in Figure 3.4.

3.10   KERNEL-PATTERN 5

INTRANSITIVE VERBS are ones that may not be followed by objects, for example, *arrive, disappear, even-*

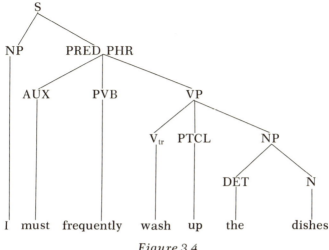

Figure 3.4

tuate, glow, happen, occur, sleep, vanish, tremble. They, too, can be followed by prepositional phrases that are attached closely to the verb:

The man disappeared *into the dark*
We arrived *at the airport*

Again, these are to be distinguished from place and time adverbials that can be loosely attached at the end of any sentence, for example, *The man disappeared on Monday.*

Finally, notice that adverbials of manner can occur in Pattern 5:

The man disappeared into the dark in a mysterious way

A sample of Pattern 5 is shown in Figure 3.5.

3.11 KERNEL-PATTERN 6

Certain verbs, including those which refer to the experiencing of sense-impressions, may be followed by

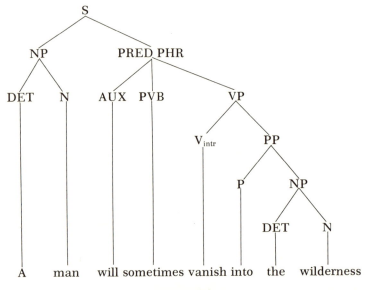

Figure 3.5

adjectives, for example, *feel, smell, taste, look, sound, seem, become, turn, stay.* The last three could not really be described as verbs of sensation, but we will use the label SENSE-VERBS to cover the group. The label must simply be regarded as a loose one.

In this pattern, as in other positions where adjectives occur, a single-wood adjective may be replaced by a construct consisting of intensifier + adjective.

Some sentences that conform to Pattern 6 are the following:

> The girl looked pretty
> The child felt sick (in the afternoon)
> A man was looking very sad
> The terminal must often seem busy

Figure 3.6 illustrates the last sentence.

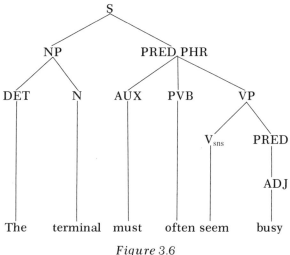

Figure 3.6

3.12 KERNEL-PATTERN 7

The sense-verbs cited in Pattern 6 can also be followed by noun phrases so as to make predicative statements. In this they somewhat resemble the verb BE, but in other ways they are different. The noun phrase may or may not be preceded by the word *like*. Some sentences that illustrate the pattern are these:

> I felt a fool
> She looked like a successful soprano
> It seemed an unlikely story

Patterns 6 and 7, involving sense-verbs, are like Patterns 1 and 2, except that those involve BE instead. The reader may wonder at first glance why BE and SNS VERB are presented in separate patterns when the patterns in which they appear are the same. The reason is that they participate in different transformations. For example, a sentence containing BE can be involved in the deletion shown at the end of Section 5.6, but one containing SNS VERB cannot.

Note that there is a difference of structure between *She looked like a successful soprano* and *She ate like a successful soprano.* The former is an example of Pattern 7, but the latter is an example of Pattern 3, with *like a successful soprano* acting as a MANNER AV. See Figure 3.7 for an example.

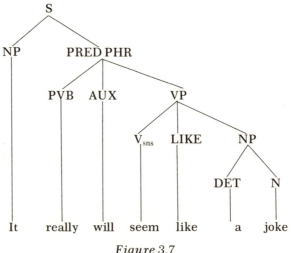

Figure 3.7

4
NUMBER
AND AGREEMENT

4.1 THE CONCEPT OF MORPHEMES

One of the more important concepts in modern language theory has been that of the MORPHEME, and, although the grammatical procedures followed in this book are not heavily dependent on it, some use will be made of it. A morpheme has been variously defined, but the simplest notion for our purposes is that it is the smallest meaningful linguistic unit. So the word *typewriter* (/taypraytər/) has three morphemes: *type* (/tayp/), *write* (/rayt/), and *-er* (/ər/). The meaning of *-er* is something like "that which does the action named in the preceding syllables."

It would be easy to be misled by this example into thinking that morphemes were identical with syllables, but that is not so. The word *hotel*, which contains two syllables, contains only one morpheme, since it cannot meaningfully be broken down into smaller parts. The word *cats* (/kæts/), on the other hand, consists of only one syllable, but contains two morphemes: *cat* (/kæt/) and *-s* (/s/).

We could become a great deal more technical about morphemes, but for the purposes before us it is not necessary to do so. The grammatical description given here is concerned mainly with words, and no great amount of theory is necessary to understand the few references that will be made to morphemes.

4.2   NUMBER IN NOUNS

Consider the simple kernel-type sentence *Frogs jump.* The single word that constitutes the noun phrase, *frogs*, is made up of two morphemes: *frog*   frɔg/) and *-s* (/z/). The first morpheme is really the carrier of the dictionary meaning of the word, but the /z/ conveys the idea of plurality. Sometimes it is said that /frɔg/ has lexical meaning, while /z/ has structural meaning. The morpheme /frɔg/ is found in only a few English words, such as *frogman* and *leapfrog.* It is limited in its distribution and could not be described as occurring as a regular feature of English structure. But /z/ could. It can occur, with its meaning of plurality, as the last morpheme in most English nouns. It is therefore a regular part of English structure. Some nouns have a slightly different form of this morpheme on the end to express plurality. Sometimes the spelling is *-es*, and sometimes the pronunciation (for either spelling) is /s/ or /əz/.

We are so used to thinking in terms of spelling that many people are not aware of any difference of sound between the plural endings on *frogs* and on *books*, or between either of those and the one on *judges;* but if we wrote the words phonemically, they would be /frɔgz/, /buks/, and /ǰəǰəz/. Note that if we compare the spelling of the singular word *judge* with that of the plural, *judges*, we see a difference of only one letter, *-s*; but if we compare the sounds, the difference is /əz/. On other occasions, an ending with this sound will be supplied by the addition of *-es* in the spelling, as in *box* — *boxes* (/baks/ — /baksəz/). We may sum up the situation by saying that there are two spellings, *-s* and *-es*, and three pronunciations, /s/, /z/, and /əz/. All indicate plurality, and all are regarded as belonging to the same morpheme, which may be represented as /ES/. The technical way of describing this is to say that they are ALLOMORPHS of the same morpheme, that is to say, alternative members of the same morpheme.

This description of plural forms will suffice for the great majority of English nouns, but there is just a handful of exceptional ones, which do not form their plurals in this way. However, the remaining plural forms occur in the same structural contexts as do nouns with an /ES/ plural, and so we are able to group them all together. Let us have a look at the main types of exceptions:

thief — thieves
The difference between singular and plural here involves not only the addition of the /ES/ morpheme but also the change from /f/ to /v/ in the stem. There are other words that follow this pattern, such as *wife — wives, wolf — wolves, scarf — scarves*.

child — children
So far as the written language is concerned, the difference between singular and plural here is the addition of *-ren;* but in the spoken language there is also a change in the stem of the word

from the diphthong /aɪ/ to the vowel /ɪ/. This is virtually the only word that ends this way. *Ox –oxen* and the archaic *brother–brethren* are rather similar.

tooth–teeth
Here, there is an altogether different way of indicating the plural. No endings are involved, only a change in the middle part of the words *tooth –teeth*. Others are *foot–feet, man–men, woman –women, goose–geese*.

mouse–mice
This item also shows internal change, but, in addition, the letter *s* is changed to *c* in the spelling. (Notice that both letters stand for the same sound in pronunciation.)

There are some words that have the same form in the plural as the singular, such as *fish–fish* (though the plural *fishes* is used occasionally), *sheep–sheep, salmon–salmon, head–head* (of cattle), *stone–stone* (weight). Many terms used in measurement of one kind or another tend to have unchanged plurals. Notice that many people say, "It's three *foot* long." Many others prefer to say, "It's three *feet* long," but the same ones will say, "It's three *foot* six," and will refer to "a three-*foot* rule." Usage has not yet become fixed.

It is well known that the English language has a capacity for borrowing words from other languages and that it often "swallows them whole"–that is, takes them over in the exact form they had in their original languages. Often the form of the plural is taken over at first from the donor-language, and so there are in English numerous non-English plural forms.

Fungus—fungi and *curriculum—curricula* are from Latin; *concerto—concerti* from Italian; *trousseau —trousseaux* from French, and so on. Words are especially likely to preserve their original plurals while they are new to English; but, after a time, anglicized plurals are often invented for them, and these may compete for survival with the borrowed form. So, alongside *fungi, curricula, concerti*, and *trousseaux* are the anglicized plurals, *funguses, curriculums, concertos*, and *trousseaus.* Indeed, the anglicized forms are now more often used than the foreign forms, in these four words.

Sometimes, we make both foreign and anglicized forms permanent in the language by giving them different functions. *Index* has two plurals in English: *indices*, the original Latin form, is preferred by mathematicians to describe the powers to which given quantities are raised, while *indexes*, the anglicized form, is normally used by librarians and others to refer to the alphabetical lists of references found at the ends of books. There is a similar differentiation of usage between the two plurals of *appendix:* doctors tend to talk about *vermiform appendices*, whereas librarians and others talk of *appendixes of books.*

There are several words in English in which the two separate elements each traditionally take a plural: *lord-justice—lords-justices: man-servant—men-servants.* However, both words are used so rarely by the average person that the ability to form such esoteric plurals is the privilege of the highly literate. *Man-servants* or *lord-justices* would neither surprise nor dismay most ears.

Some compound expressions of French origin have an

adjective following a noun, in contrast to the usual English order of adjective + noun. In such expressions, the plural ending has traditionally been attached to the element that was originally a French noun: *court-martial — courts-martial; Governor-general — Governors-general.* However, there is a growing tendency to think of the whole expression as a noun in English, and to forget or ignore the origins of the elements; so many people would not hesitate to say *court-martials, Governor-generals.* This tendency has long since triumphed in such English nouns as *handfuls, spoonfuls, bucketfuls.*

Some words that are already plural in form come to be treated as singulars, and then another plural indication is added: *threepence,* already a plural form in origin, comes to be used in phrases like *a threepence* (because the coin representing that value is a single object), and consequently a new plural, *threepences,* is formed. *Dice,* originally the plural of *die,* is often used as if it were a singular. The plural is then either left the same (*dice*) or formed with the regular plural-forming element *-s* (/əz/). On the other hand, some words that were originally singular have been mistaken for plurals, and other singulars derived from them. The word *peas* was originally singular, but the /z/ ending was mistakenly comprehended as a plural inflection, and the new singular, *pea,* derived.

Some words, like *gallows, scissors, news, means,* have no plural form, and, where it is necessary to show plurality, it is done by a phrase: *pairs of scissors, pieces of news,* etc. For obvious reasons, it is usually only words standing for countable objects that have plurals. There are others, such as *steel, grass, hair, sugar,* and *dirt,* which, in most contexts, are used as

MASS-NOUNS; that is, the concept of counting does not apply to them. There are also abstract nouns, such as *love, hunger*, and *pain*, which are not usually found in the plural. It is only COUNT-NOUNS that must have a determiner when they occur in the singular. Some of the same words that occur as mass-nouns also occur in different contexts as count-nouns. So we say "I had my *hair* cut," but "I just pulled out two *hairs*"; "He cut the *grass*," but "He tried planting several different *grasses*."

It should be noted that proper nouns are rarely found in plural form. We sometimes do pluralize them for special effects: "*Churchills* are found only once in an epoch"; "I'd like to buy a few *Dobells*."

The question as to whether a noun phrase will be considered as singular or plural for the purposes of correlation with the rest of a sentence is not answered purely by the form of words. As is well known, collective nouns like *team, committee*, and *crowd* are singular in form but are variously treated as singular or plural, according to the feeling of the speaker. Modern grammarians decline to lay down hard-and-fast rules about what number such a word *ought* to be. Rather similar is the problem of the number of partitive genitives, that is to say, phrases like *a bundle of newspapers*. It is likely that this expression would be regarded as singular, but a more difficult choice must be made with *none of my friends*. The word on which the decision rests is *none*. In form the word is singular, and its literal meaning of *not one* is conventionally taken to be support for this notion; however, many speakers when using a phrase like *none of my friends* think of the phrase as being the negative form of *all of my friends* or *some of my friends*, and so treat the phrase as plural. Likewise, *each of us* is often thought of as being equivalent to *all of us* and therefore regarded as plural. Only personal preference can decide such issues.

4.3 AUXILIARIES IN KERNEL SENTENCES

Earlier, it was pointed out that the item AUXILIARY in a kernel-pattern could be a sequence of words, and it was suggested that the relevant formula was:

$$(\text{MODAL}) + (\text{HAVE}) + (\text{BE})$$

This formula may be interpreted as follows: an item from each of the three types may be selected in turn in the order shown. The parentheses indicate that in each case it is optional whether a choice is made or not.

When a Modal Is First

There are no restrictions on the choice of a modal: any item from the list may be chosen, or none may be. If a modal is chosen, then only one form of HAVE may follow, and that is *have* itself. On the other hand, HAVE may be omitted. If it is, then *be* is the only form that can be chosen from the third type. If HAVE is chosen, the only form of BE that can follow it is *been*. On the other hand, both HAVE and BE may be omitted. These possibilities may be summed up thus:

$$\text{MODAL} + (\left\{ \begin{array}{l} have \ + \ (been) \\ be \end{array} \right\})$$

This gives us auxiliary sequences like *will have been, might be*.

When HAVE *Is First*

If no modal at all is chosen, and a form of HAVE is selected, the choice is made from *have, has,* and *had* according to two criteria:

a. If the present form of this auxiliary is required, the choice must be either *has* or *have,* the choice being determined by the form of the subject. As far as noun-subjects go, the pattern is simple: singular nouns are followed by *has,* and plural ones by *have.* Pronoun-subjects are a little more complicated: all the plural pronouns are followed by *have,* but so are the singluars *I* and *you.* Only *he, she,* and *it* are followed by *has.*

b. If the past form of this auxiliary is required, *had* is chosen regardless of the form of the subject.

When BE *Is First*

Sometimes, neither a modal nor a form of HAVE is selected, so that a form of BE is the first item in the auxiliary. Once again, the choice is made according to two criteria:

a. If the present form is required, the choice must be from *am, is, are.* Noun-subjects are again quite straightforward: singulars are followed by *is* and plurals by *are.* But, once again, the pronouns are more complicated: the plural pronouns are all followed by *are,* and so is the singular *you. I* is uniquely followed by *am. He, she,* and *it* are followed by *is.*

b. If the past form is required, the choice is between *was* and *were.* Singular nouns and all singular pronouns except *you* are associated with *was*, and all plural nouns and pronouns and the singular *you* are associated with *were*.

Let us sum up the facts just outlined. The first item appearing in the auxiliary agrees with the subject: that is, correlates in form with it. The details of the correlation may be summarized as in Table 4.1.

Table 4.1

Sing nouns + *he, she, it*	A	A	*has, is*
I	B	B	*am*
Plur nouns + *you, we, they*	C	C	*are, were*
		AB	*was*
		BC	*have*
		ABC	*had*, MODALS

In this table, the letters to the right of the items in the subject represent the three different types. A = all singulars except *I* and *you*; B = *I*; and C = all plurals and *you* (singular or plural). The correlations of these with an initial auxiliary may be found by matching these letters with the ones to the left of the auxiliaries. So we find that *is* and *has* correlate only with subjects of type A, *am* only with B, *are* and *were* only with C, *was* with both A and B, *have* with both B and C, while *had* and the modals correlate with A, B, and C.

The facts presented here are meant to be a description of educated usage. Not all people in the community use these sets of correlations in exactly the form presented, and it is not implied that the ones described here are *intrinsically* better than any other sets. They are, however, more acceptable *socially* (see Section 4.5).

4.4 AGREEMENT BETWEEN SUBJECT AND VERB

When a verb cluster contains both auxiliary and verb, the verb always follows the auxiliary, never precedes it. Furthermore, the verb agrees with the subject only when there is no auxiliary; or, to put it another way, whichever of these two classes stands at the beginning of the verb cluster agrees with the subject.

The correlations of verbs with head-words of subjects may be summarized as shown in Table 4.2. It will be noticed that two types of verbs are tabled: *wants* and *gives*, each of which stands for a host of verbs. The two are known as weak and strong verbs respectively, and they trace their ancestry back to two different types of conjugations in Old English. Weak verbs are those that have an ending for the past tense pronounced /əd/ as in *wanted*, /d/ as in *loved*, or /t/ as in *laughed*. These three endings are regarded as the same morpheme, which we may call the /ED/ morpheme. Strong verbs do not use this system to show past tense, but change their internal vowels like *give* − *gave*.

Table 4.2

Sing nouns + *he, she, it*	A	A	*wants, gives*
	I B	BC	*want, give*
Plur nouns + *you, we, they*	C	ABC	*wanted, gave*

4.5 AGREEMENT BETWEEN AUXILIARY AND VERB

We have already seen how auxiliaries and verbs correlate with subjects, when they are in the leading position of a verb-cluster. But when the cluster consists of AUXILIARY + VERB, the first item in the auxiliary agrees with the subject, while the verb agrees with the last item in the auxiliary (whether this is first, second, or third in order). Agreements of this latter kind follow the pattern shown in Table 4.3. The correlations should be read straight across, line by line. This table does not include passive forms of the verb, which are derived later by transformation.

Table 4.3

Last auxiliary	Main verb
MODAL *have, has, had* *am, is, are, was, were, be, been*	*want, give* *wanted, given* *wanting, giving*

The agreements shown in this and the two preceding sections are not learned as tables by native speakers, of course, but are picked up by children imitating the usage of their elders. Eventually, the correlations that have been learned over a long period, and with many errors and corrections, become unconscious knowledge. When mistakes occur in the correlations, it usually means, not that learning has been imperfect, but that the correlations normally made by the adults in the community where the individual grew up are different from those used by the so-called "educated" speakers of the language. The forms *wanted* and *given* are often called past participles of their respective verbs. But many speakers do not make this correlation; they tend to use either *give* or *gave* in the position where "educated" speakers would use *given: I ought to have give him a hiding; I ought to have gave him a hiding.* In discussions on horse racing, the expression *He couldn't be beat* can easily be heard, instead of the

more "educated" *He couldn't be beaten.* The trouble is
not that the speaker "isn't using a participle" but that
his participle is different from the one accepted as the
prestige form. The reasons for rejecting *beat* in favor
of *beaten* have little to do with the intrinsic merits of
the two forms; they are a matter of fashion. It happens to be the case that nearly all educated speakers,
and a good many others, use *beaten* and *given* for the
past participles, and that means that it is socially necessary to adopt these forms unless one wants to be
thought uneducated.

Now, because the reason for recommending one
form rather than another is social and not linguistic, it
does not follow that it does not matter which form you
use. Social pressures are very strong, and anyone who
thought he could ignore them would be mistaken. Of
course, it is possible for someone to conduct a purpose-
ful revolution against a convention that he feels is
harmful in some way; but this particular convention of
the language is no more harmful than any other choice
would be, and the effort that would be required to
change it would be out of proportion to the merit of any
possible result. Let us accept, then, that it is desirable
for an educated person to use the form *beaten* rather
than *beat* for the past participle. It is clear that a teacher
has every right to teach this fact to his pupils — indeed,
he has an obligation to do so.

5
SOME BASIC
SENTENCE VARIATIONS

5.1 INTRODUCTION

The kernel sentences described in Chapter 3 should be thought of as the nucleus of English structure. We can describe other sentence-types by reference to this nucleus, and that is exactly what is to be done in this chapter and the ones to follow. In particular, we are going to study what changes must be wrought on the structures of kernel sentences to convert them into new structures. The changes may be referred to as "transformations." In a later chapter, some account will be given of the technical use of this word by formal linguists, but for the moment we may use the word with the simple meaning just described. The reader will recognize most of the raw material of these chapters as being familiar enough, but the particular relationships and their organization are based on the insights of generative grammar. One of the virtues aimed at here is that of presenting material in a form that could be transmitted to beginners, but that would also form a convenient basis for later work at a higher linguistic level. Transformational grammar, as known to specialists in the field, is too technical to be suitable for purposes such as this book is meant to serve; but the insights of linguistics can be presented here in an informal way that parallels that of a more technical description. Those who later study the more technical accounts should find their task easier after following the general direction of the account in this simplified form. Let us begin with the most familiar transformation of all.

5.2 THE SEPARATION TRANSFORMATION

Transformations are changes wrought on sentence structure; they may add items, delete them, or simply alter the order in which they occur. The simplest to illustrate is what Chomsky has called the separation transformation:

He *tore up* the paper → He *tore* the paper *up*

The first sentence is simply an instance of Kernel-Pattern 4; the second is derived through a simple ORDER-CHANGE, involving the particle and the NP that follows it.

This particular transformation is generally optional; it is a matter of choice whether we say *He tore up the paper* or make the transformation to *He tore the paper up*. There is a special case when the object is a pronoun, for then the transformation becomes obligatory. We cannot say **I sent away him*, but we can say *I sent him away*. On the other hand, we can say either *I sent away a letter* or *I sent a letter away*.

---

*The asterisk is used here and throughout to signify a sentence that is not satisfactory.

Notice that the combination of verb + particle in the first sentence has a meaning different from that of the verb by itself. If someone tears my paper, I can perhaps still read it, but if he tears it up, I probably can't. Other combinations of the same kind are: *wash up, wash down, throw out, give up, put down, win over, tidy up*, and *take on*. These are only a few of hundreds. It will be noticed that the particle often has not its specific dictionary meaning; it often has a very vague meaning, as in *wash up.*

5.3 THE IMPERATIVE TRANSFORMATION

The sort of transformation with which we are concerned at the moment is applied to a base whose structure either is, or is similar to, that of a kernel-pattern. In the transformation just illustrated, the base was *identical* with the structure of a kernel-pattern. We are now going to study a number of cases where the base is *similar* to a kernel but has one or more additional elements.

A transformation is conceived of as a change in structure not involving any change in meaning, and so the base always includes all the elements of meaning that are to be present in the final sentence. In the separation transformation, it so happened that one of the kernel-patterns was sufficient base in itself, since it already contained all the meaning that was to be present after the change. But, in other cases, there are more elements in the base than just a simple kernel-pattern.

One case in point is the imperative transformation. The changes that it brings about are of this kind:

IMP + You will go to the shop → Go to the shop

The item IMP here carries the meaning "imperative," that is, *the speaker requests that* . . . or something similar. We include this item IMP on the left-hand side to balance the equation of meaning. To put it another way, the meaning of the elements on the left is realized in the form shown on the right.

Any kernel sentence beginning *You will* . . . can combine with IMP to form the base for this transformation. What happens is that the items IMP + *You will* are deleted from the base. Or, if we prefer, we may delete only IMP + *will*, since *You go to the shop* is an acceptable imperative sentence. The whole transformation is optional, since *You will go to the shop* can be a kind of imperative in its own right, and not just a future tense.

The reader may feel that an imperative could be related to any sentence with *you* as the subject, but there are good reasons for preferring to associate it only with *will.* Tag-questions tacked on to sentences usually show the same structure as the sentence they are attached to, and on imperative sentences we find only tag-questions containing *will:*

> Go to the shop, will you?
> *not* *Go to the shop, must you?

Of course, there are some sentences, even of the right pattern, that are never converted into imperatives. We do not find:

*Believe in fairies
*Want my car
*Feel well

5.4   THE PASSIVE TRANSFORMATION

Every native speaker of English feels that there is some relationship between the two sentences *The conductor started the bus* and *The bus was started by the conductor.* We are conscious of many pairs of sentences that are related in this way. For example:

1. The conductor starts the bus
   The bus is started by the conductor
2. The conductor has started the bus
   The bus has been started by the conductor
3. The conductor is starting the bus
   The bus is being started by the conductor
4. The conductor has been starting the bus
   *The bus has been being started by the conductor
5. The conductor started the bus
   The bus was started by the conductor
6. The conductor had started the bus
   The bus had been started by the conductor
7. The conductor was starting the bus
   The bus was being started by the conductor
8. The conductor had been starting the bus
   *The bus had been being started by the conductor
9. The conductor will start the bus
   The bus will be started by the conductor
10. The conductor will have started the bus
    The bus will have been started by the conductor
11. The conductor will be starting the bus
    *The bus will be being started by the conductor

12. The conductor will have been starting the bus
    *The bus will have been being started by the
    conductor

The sentences marked with an asterisk are passives
that would be most unlikely to occur. Yet everyone will
agree that, if such passives did occur, these are the
forms they would take. We must have some unconscious formula for constructing passives.

Taking the first of these for illustration, we might set
out the relevant passive transformation like this:

The conductor starts the bus + by PASSIVE
$\longrightarrow$ The bus is started by the conductor

Once again, we have seen to it that all the elements of
meaning are expressed in the base, from which the
passive is derived by structural change only. Let us
now try to express in an organized way what is involved in that change.

   a. The object noun phrase (*the bus*) moves
around and replaces the subject noun phrase (*the
conductor*). The latter, in turn, takes the place of
the item PASSIVE, which is then deleted.
   b. If any auxiliaries occur in the active, they are
carried over to the passive unaltered.
   c. Part of the verb BE is introduced. If there is an
auxiliary which has been brought over from the
active, BE occurs after it, according to the following selection plan:
      i. After *have, has,* or *had,* it takes the form *been.*
     ii. After *am, is, are, was, were, be,* or *been,* it
         takes the form *being.*
    iii. After *will* or any other modal auxiliary, it
         takes the form *be.*

d. If there is no auxiliary brought over from the active form, the part of BE now introduced will show tense and number indication (and person, where the subject is a pronoun). See Sentences 1 and 5 at the beginning of this section.

e. The part of BE mentioned in *c* and *d* will in every case be followed by the past participle of the same verb that occurred in the active sentence.

The passive transformation can be effected only in sentences that contain certain verbs, not all of them. Chomsky points out that there are some — the so-called "middle verbs" — that do not take adverbials of manner freely, and that these same ones are not associated with the passive transformation. They include *cost (The book cost four dollars)*, *weigh (The parcel weighed seven pounds)*, and *resemble (My father resembles the Prime Minister)*. In general it is true that the verbs that can freely take adverbs of manner can also be involved in the passive transformation, but even they can be immutable in some contexts. The verbs in the following sentences would often be subject to a passive change, but in these specific contexts are not:

The man minded his own business
The two friends shook hands
We changed buses

It is often said that in the active form of a sentence the subject expresses the "*doer*" of the action, and the object expresses the "receiver" of it, while in the passive it is the subject that is the receiver of the action. This is often so, but not always. For example, in *The boy fears the teacher*, it can hardly be said that *the teacher* stands for the receiver of any action; and in the passive form *The teacher is feared by the boy*, the subject (*The teacher*) can hardly be said to be the receiver of the action, either. The difference between the active and the passive is primarily one of form and structure, rather than of meaning, but it is true that there is a strong tendency toward the correlations with meaning that are traditionally cited.

A passive sentence such as *The bus was started by the conductor* can occur with the agent-phrase deleted and still often make a sensible sentence: *The bus was started*. This only means that we have a partial of the full passive pattern. Notice that *The bus was started* is the passive not of *The bus started* (though the meanings come close to being an active/passive contrast), but of (*Someone*) *started the bus*.

5.5 THE FORMATION OF INDIRECT OBJECTS

In certain circumstances, a prepositional phrase that follows a transitive verb and begins with *to* or *for* can be transformed into an indirect object. This is the Modern English way of expressing a relationship which in Old English and Latin was expressed by the dative case. For the transformation to apply, one of a limited subset of verbs must occur in the sentence, for example, *give, lend, offer, send, build, buy, get, leave, make*. Some of these are associated with *to* (*give, lend, offer, send*) and some with *for* (*build, buy, get, leave, make*).

Let us deal first with constructions involving *to:*

He offered a cigarette to me
⟶ He offered me a cigarette

Notice that the transformation would not apply to such

sentences as *I charged the book to my account*, or *I drove the car to Sydney*, because their verbs do not belong to the special subset.

The transformation just illustrated belongs logically before the application of the passive transformation, since the latter can apply to the sentence resulting from the transformation, as well as the one to which it is applied. In other words, the passive transformation can be applied to either *He offered a cigarette to me* or *He offered me a cigarette.* If we apply it to the first, here is what happens:

> He offered a cigarette to me
> ⟶ A cigarette was offered to me by him

The phrase *by him* can be optionally deleted. Now, if we apply the passive transformation to *He offered me a cigarette*, there are two possible results:

> He offered me a cigarette
> ⟶ I was offered a cigarette
> *or* A cigarette was offered me

Now let us see what happens in sentences where the prepositional phrase begins with *for*:

> He bought an ice cream for me
> ⟶ He bought me an ice cream

This transformation, unlike the one for sentences with *to*, belongs logically *after* the application of the passive transformation, since its resultant sentences are not subject to the passive change.

5.6 DELETIONS

Certain transitive verbs can appear either with or without objects. In transformational grammar, the full pattern, including the object, is presented, and then the deletion is made. So the shorter sentence is regarded as a truncated version of the longer one, rather than the longer one being regarded as an extension of the shorter one:

I smoke cigarettes ⟶ I smoke
She washes clothes ⟶ She washes
He reads books ⟶ He reads

Although these examples are presented in the form of specific sentences, for the purpose of conveying the concept clearly, the deletion applies, not to any such overt words, but to the structural pattern underlying them. The example might be more accurately shown in this form:

NP + TR VERB + NP ⟶ NP + TR VERB

Since part of a *pattern* is deleted, and not merely specific words, it is clear that deletions involve a somewhat different notion from the conventional one of "words understood," and that the objections to these are irrelevant here.

In another kind of deletion, a sequence consisting of auxiliary + verb can be reduced to the auxiliary alone; that is,

NP + AUX + VERB ⟶ NP + AUX
He does teach ⟶ He does
I can swim ⟶ I can
John hasn't finished ⟶ John hasn't
The book isn't torn ⟶ The book isn't

Similarly, a deletion can occur when there is BE followed by an adjective; that is,

NP + BE + ADJ $\longrightarrow$ NP + BE
My car isn't new $\longrightarrow$ My car isn't

These deletions obviously occur only in situations where the deleted word is unnecessary, since its meaning is provided either by the rest of the conversation or by the physical context. Note that, in several of these examples, the item NEG has been added to both sequences.

5.7 QUESTIONS INVOLVING *WHO, WHICH,* AND *WHAT*

There are several different kinds of questions in English, but we will begin with the so-called WH-QUESTIONS. Many of the words that are used to ask questions happen to begin with the letters *wh: who, whom, whose, which, what, when, where, why.* The notable exception is *how,* but the fact that it doesn't strictly qualify on spelling is ignored, and it is called a *wh*-word, too. So we are concerned with questions that begin with one such word.

Here is a sample question transformation, which will serve as an illustration of several matters:

Q + <u>The thing</u> fell on his head
     WH

$\longrightarrow$ Which thing fell on his head?

The symbol Q means "question" and indicates that a question is to be asked about the sentence that follows. But it is not the whole statement that is to be queried; it is only *the thing* about which more information is sought. The fact that this is the queried item is shown by the letters WH beneath, and the effect of the transformation is to replace the determiner by a *wh*-word.

Now, for comparison, look at this example:

Q + The secretary has lost <u>the thing</u>
                                  WH

$\longrightarrow$ Which thing has the secretary lost?

Here it is not the subject but the object that is queried, and the resultant sentence is correspondingly different. We may summarize what happens as follows:

    a. The queried noun phrase is brought to the front of the sentence.

    b. The definite article *the* is changed to a *wh*-word, namely, *which*.

    c. The subject and the auxiliary change places.

    d. The symbol Q is deleted.

Note that only *b* and *d* happen when it is the subject that is queried. But *a* does not need to happen, since the item is already at the front of the sentence.

The question arises: What happens when a sentence does not contain an auxiliary? How is *c* in the preceding paragraph carried out? To be specific, how do we effect the transformation in this case?

Q + The secretary lost <u>the thing</u>
                              WH

We can move the noun phrase to the front of the sentence, and change the word *the* to *which*, but when we come to inverting the subject and the auxiliary, we find ourselves in a dilemma, for no auxiliary appears in the simple past. The reader well knows, from his own experience as a speaker of the language, what is done in these circumstances:

a. A part of the word DO is introduced as a kind of dummy auxiliary, and it is invested with any indications of tense and number that were previously carried by the verb.

b. The verb is reduced to its unchanged form (*lose*).

c. The dummy auxiliary changes place with the subject, just as any other auxiliary does in the formation of this sort of question.

We can now complete our formulation of the change:

Q + The secretary lost <u>the thing</u>
                        WH
⟶ Which thing did the secretary lose?

It is not suggested that a native speaker of English, either consciously or unconsciously, goes through these steps in quite this way. The description merely formulates the principles involved.

When a *wh*-word appears without an accompanying noun (*Who will ask him? What will he do?*), the base contains a noun phrase with an indefinite article. For the purpose of this description, we must regard *some* as an indefinite article and *someone* as a noun phrase containing an indefinite article (just as if *some* and *one* were written as separate words). The connection between such a base and such a question is illustrated in the examples that follow:

Q + <u>Someone</u> will invite Barry
       WH
⟶ Who will invite Barry?

Q + Barry will invite <u>someone</u>
                            WH

⟶ Who(m) will Barry invite?

Notice that, in the second of these, where the queried element is an object, the same steps are carried out as before:

a. The queried noun phrase is brought to the front of the sentence.

b. The noun phrase is changed to a *wh*-word, namely, *whom* (or, in the speech of many people, *who*).

c. The subject and the auxiliary are inverted.

d. The symbol Q is deleted.

Parallel to all the questions deriving *who* from *someone* are those that derive *what* from *something*:

Q + <u>Something</u> fell out of the car
      WH

⟶ What fell out of the car?

Q + The President should say <u>something</u>
                                   WH

⟶ What should the President say?

5.8 OTHER WH-QUESTIONS

The transformations that produce questions containing the words *when*, *where*, *why*, and *how* are similar to the ones that produce those containing *who* and *what*.

Q + Rain has been falling at <u>some place</u>
                                  WH

⟶ At what place has rain been falling?

In this transformation, the same steps as before have been carried out, namely:

    a. The queried element has been brought to the front of the sentence.

    b. Some has been changed to a *wh*-word, *what.*

    c. The subject and the auxiliary have been inverted.

    d. The symbol Q has been deleted.

The phrase *at some place* is a place adverbial, and this particular base sentence belongs to Kernel-Pattern 5. (However, any of the kernel-patterns can be involved.)

In some informal use of language, it is not the whole phrase that is moved to the front but just the noun phrase, so that the resultant sentence is *What place has rain been falling at (or in)?*

There is a further step that is nearly always carried out, as the reader may already have remarked to himself: *at what place* is usually replaced by *where,* to produce *Where has rain been falling?*

Questions involving *when* are derived in a similar way:

    Q + The concert will begin <u>at some time</u>

                                    WH

⟶ At what time will the concert begin?

⟶ When will the concert begin?

The origin of *why* questions is similar:

    Q + the man was dismissed <u>for some reason</u>

                                    WH

⟶ For what reason was the man dismissed?

⟶ Why was the man dismissed?

Also, *how* questions are parallel:

Q + The accident happened <u>in some way</u>
$$\text{WH}$$
$\longrightarrow$ In what way did the accident happen?
$\longrightarrow$ How did the accident happen?

5.9 QUESTIONS REQUIRING A *YES/NO* ANSWER

There are some questions that are a little different from those we have just been examining, notably, those which invite a *yes* or *no* answer. These do not begin with a *wh*-word. It is the whole sentence that is queried in these, so we may show the transformation thus:

Q + The winner can choose a prize
$\longrightarrow$ Can the winner choose a prize?

The transformation is simpler than the ones we have already examined. Here there is no element to be changed to a *wh*-word, and none to be brought to the front of the sentence. All that happens is that the subject and the auxiliary are reversed and the symbol Q is deleted. Once again, where there is no auxiliary, a form of DO is introduced as a dummy auxiliary:

Q + He knows the truth
$\longrightarrow$ Does he know the truth?

6
GENERALIZED
BASES

Sometimes the base for a sentence is made up of two or more kernel-patterns. If one simply follows the other, they are said to be "conjoined":

$$[S_1] \quad]S_2]$$

On the other hand, if one is included within the other, it is said to be "embedded" in it:

$$[S_1 \quad [S_2] \quad S_1]$$

In this section, we will examine the process of conjoining. The double kernel-pattern from which the conjoined sentence is derived is called a GENERALIZED BASE. Here is an example:

[Helen has come to the party]   [John has gone to a film]
(Kernel-Pattern 5)   (Kernel-Pattern 5)

Now, a sequence such as this is merely the base for a conjoined sentence; it is not the sentence. To convert it into sentence form, one of a number of transformations is applied. In this case, our ultimate aim is a sentence in which the two elements are joined by *and*. We might describe the transformation in these terms:

$$[S_1] \quad [S_2] \longrightarrow [S_1] \ and \ [S_2]$$

That is,

[Helen has come to the party] [John has gone to a film]
$\longrightarrow$ Helen has come to the party *and* John has gone to a film

It so happens that both elements here are instances of Kernel-Pattern 5, but this is not a necessary condition. Almost any two kernel-pattern types can be conjoined; but it is important to say any *types*, and not any individual sentences. For instance, it is unlikely that these two sequences would be conjoined, even though their kernel-patterns are compatible with joining:

[I've sugared my tea] [de Gaulle has been re-elected]

When the elements of a generalized base are the same except for their subjects, we may join them by enclosing the second in *and . . . too.*

[Helen has come to the party] [John has come to the party]
$\longrightarrow$ Helen has come to the party *and* John has come to the party *too*

The resultant sentence here is more theoretically possible than likely, for speakers usually delete some part of the second element that is mere repetition of the first. This is also a transformation.

Helen has come *to the party* and John has come *to the party* too
⟶ Helen has come *to the party* and John has come too

Often the deletion is carried further, so that all repetitious words except one are deleted.

Helen has *come* to the party and John has *come* too
⟶ Helen has *come* to the party and John has too

And even that one word is dispensable.

Helen *has* come to the party and John *has* too
⟶ Helen *has* come to the party and John too

The second element in the base can be abbreviated in various ways in the output sentence; it is not always simply a matter of deletion.

[Bill saw the concert]   [Harry saw the concert]
⟶ Bill saw the concert and Harry saw the concert too
⟶ Bill saw the concert and Harry saw *it* too

Here, repetition of the object noun phrase has been avoided by substituting *it*, a pronoun.

Another possibility is for the last line of the preceding to take this form:

Bill saw the concert and Harry *did* too

Here, a process has occurred which is similar to certain ones described earlier: a dummy auxiliary has been introduced.

In this case, the verb accompanying the dummy auxiliary is altered to the "central" form *see*, but for the purposes of deletion it is still "the same word" as *saw*.

Both *saw* and *did see* are merely different surface forms of a deep-structure sequence PAST + *see*.

There is yet another form that the resultant sentence can take:

Bill saw the concert *and so* did Harry

This sentence may be thought of as being derived from the *and . . . too* type, *too* being replaced by *so*, which then changes its position. But notice that when *so* is used in this way, an inversion of the rest of the clause takes place, similar to what occurs with some questions. Likewise:

My sister can ski and so *can I*
Shirley will try and so *will Betty*
Bob has graduated and so *has Stan*

6.2 RELATIVE CLAUSES

English grammars of all kinds, from conventional to transformational, have recognized the relationship between single-word adjectives, adjectival phrases, and adjectival clauses. They are often grouped together as ADJECTIVALS or adjectival modifiers. In the words of conventional grammar, they "do the same work" or "have the same function."

Transformational grammarians have been interested in studying the formation of relative clauses and showing the steps by which a sentence containing an adjectival clause can be converted to one containing an adjectival phrase, and how this in turn can be converted to one containing a single-word adjective. It is clear that adjectival modifiers are a very important part of English structure. An American scholar, Carlota

S. Smith, has made an important contribution to this part of the grammar.

Sentences containing relative clauses are derived from a base which is a sequence of several kernels, two of which have a noun in common. For example:

[I bought a *violin*] [The *violin* belonged to a concert violinist]
⟶ I bought a *violin that* belonged to a concert violinist

Notice that the noun phrase in the second kernel has been changed to a relative pronoun, *that*. This can be done because the noun that was the object of the first kernel (*violin*) is the same as the one that was the subject of the second. The two kernels are simply joined, one after the other.

It is possible to reverse the roles of the two kernels in the output sentence; that is, the one that is used for the host clause becomes the relative clause, and the one used for the relative clause becomes the host. In this case, the base is expressed in such a way as to anticipate the embedding of the relative clause within the host clause:

[The *violin* [I bought a *violin*] belonged to a concert violinist]
⟶ The *violin that* I bought belonged to a concert violinist

That has been substituted for the object noun phrase in the embedded kernel; but notice that it has been brought around to the front of the kernel, in spite of the fact that it represents the object. Things are not always so complicated. The embedded kernel may share its subject noun phrase with the other kernel:

[The *violin* [The *violin* broke] belonged to a concert violinist]
⟶ The *violin that* broke belonged to a concert violinist

That may be used to replace any nominal, whether its reference is human or not. *Which* is used only when the noun phrase has a reference that is nonhuman. *Who* is used in a similar manner when the reference is human. In the speech of some people, and in the writing of many, *who* is used only when the relevant nominal that it replaces is a subject, and *whom* is used instead when the nominal is an object. *Which*, *who*, *whom*, and *that* are known as relative pronouns or, more simply, as relatives.

6.3 RESTRICTIVE AND APPOSITIVE CLAUSES
The relative pronouns introduce two kinds of relative clause: the restrictive or defining type, and the appositive or nondefining type.

RESTRICTIVE: The man *who told me that* has left
                    the firm
APPOSITIVE: The man, *who was Irish*, seemed
                    to be upset

The restrictive clause, as the reader can see, identifies or defines the particular individual referred to in the antecedent noun, while the appositive one simply adds some information that is not an identification or a definition but is almost an aside, an additional piece of information about the preceding noun-reference.
    Some people maintain the dogma that *that* can be

used only for the restrictive type, while *which* can be used only for the appositive type:

RESTRICTIVE: The film *that* I saw is a comedy
APPOSITIVE: My house, *which* I built myself, overlooks the bay

However, the dogma is not justified by usage. It can fairly be maintained that there is a *tendency* for the distinction to be made, but there is certainly no hard-and-fast rule.

6.4 THE INFLUENCE OF DETERMINERS ON RELATIVE CLAUSES

The type of determiner that precedes a nominal word has an influence on the kind of relative clause that can follow it. It is useful, as Carlota S. Smith has pointed out, to divide determiners into three types:

UNSPECIFIED DETERMINERS
Words such as *any, all.* These can be followed by restrictive relative clauses only. That is, we can have:
   Any man who is a member can do that
   All members who wish to attend the function should stand
But we cannot have:
*Any man, who is a member, can do that
*All members, who wish to attend the function, should stand
It is the commas that make all the difference to the meaning and to the admissibility of the clause.

SPECIFIED DETERMINERS
Words such as *a, the.* These can be followed by either a restrictive or an appositive relative clause. Thus each of the following sentences is acceptable:

The detectives who have solved many crimes are to be promoted

The detectives, who have solved many crimes, are to be promoted

UNIQUE DETERMINERS

When a proper noun by itself, or in partnership with *the*, refers uniquely to one individual person or place (such as *Paul, the Nile, the Queen*), the nominal is said to contain a unique determiner. Where there is no actual manifestation of the unique determiner (as with *Paul*) this is sometimes symbolized by the sign Ø, meaning zero. Unique determiners are associated with appositive relatives only. So we can have

Paul, who is intelligent, will go far

The Nile, which is a beautiful river, flows into the Mediterranean Sea

The Queen, who has visited Australia several times, plans to come again

But, if we are to understand the clause as defining, we cannot have

*Paul who is intelligent will go far

*The Murray which is a beautiful river marks the border between Victoria and New South Wales

*The Queen who has visited Australia several times plans to come again

6.5 DELETION FROM RELATIVE CLAUSES

Sometimes, the relative pronoun or the relative pronoun + BE, or the relative pronoun + certain intransitive verbs, can be deleted from a relative clause, so as to leave a phrase standing as a modifier after the nominal. Here are some examples:

A house (that stands) on a corner is likely to be robbed

He spoke to the man (who was) on the station

The violin (which) I bought belonged to a concert violinist

I boarded the train (which was) standing at the station

At other times, deletions are not possible, because they do not leave grammatical sentences. In general, deletions can be made only if the surviving phrase contains words that indicate its relationship to the rest of the sentence. For instance, a relative that consists of *which (that, who)* + BE + NP can seldom undergo deletion:

This is the school that is the polling booth

A deletion would produce the unacceptable sentence

*This is the school the polling booth

Likewise, we cannot delete from relative clauses containing *which (that, who)* followed by a verb:

That is the violinist who led the orchestra
*That is the violinist led the orchestra

6.6 ADJECTIVAL MODIFIERS

We must now consider the special case where the relative clause forms an adjectival modifier which contains a predicative adjective. Consider these two source kernels:

[I have a violin]   [The violin is valuable]

Using the same method as before, we make the second element into an adjectival modifier. Notice that one of the source kernels must be of the form NP + BE + ADJ, and that the two elements must share a common nominal.

⟶ I have a violin which is valuable

The same procedure can be followed when the adjective has a prepositional phrase attached to it:

[I picked a rose]   [The rose was remarkable in its coloring]
⟶ I picked a rose which was remarkable in its coloring

Likewise, the adjective may have a complement beginning with an infinitive verb:

[I know a story]   [The story is sad to relate]
⟶ I know a story which is sad to relate.

6.7   DELETION IN ADJECTIVAL MODIFIERS
Transformational grammar carries out optional deletions on adjectival clauses that contain a predicative adjective. The result is sometimes a sentence in its own right and is at other times merely a transitory stage before further development. Let us apply deletions to the three sentences quoted in the preceding section.

I have a violin (which is) valuable
⟶ *I have a violin valuable

The result is not yet a sentence, but is a halfway stage in a further development. (See account of order-change in next section.)

I picked a rose (which was) remarkable in its coloring

⟶ I picked a rose remarkable in its coloring

This time, we have an acceptable sentence.

I know a story (which is) sad to relate
⟶ I know a story sad to relate

Once again, an acceptable sentence.

6.8   ORDER-CHANGE OF ADJECTIVAL MODIFIERS†

In the last section, we saw the following development:

I have a violin (which is) valuable
⟶ *I have a violin valuable

In order to make an acceptable sentence out of this, we have to effect an order-change, so that the nominal and the adjective change their relative positions:

*I have a violin valuable
⟶ I have a valuable violin

We have thus developed prenominal adjectives by the following stages from predicative adjectives:

[I have a violin]   [The violin is valuable]
⟶ I have a violin which is valuable
⟶*I have a violin valuable
⟶ I have a valuable violin

There is one important exception to the order-changing rule, If the nominal is an indefinite pronoun,

---

†The procedure followed here has been to locate all the adjectival modifiers after the noun, and later to effect an order-change where necessary to place single-word adjectives in front of the noun. It is also possible to locate them all initially in front of the noun, and then later to move the phrases and clauses around to the other side of the noun, as has been done in some recent expositions of transformational grammar.

such as *anything, anybody, anyone, something, some-body, someone, everything, everybody, everyone,* the order-change is not carried out, for such words take adjectival modification following rather than preceding:

I know someone who is psychic
⟶ I know someone psychic

I can recommend something that is invaluable in a crisis
⟶ I can recommend something invaluable in a crisis

Finally, there is an optional change that applies to an adjectival modifier consisting of an adjective + complement, for example,

We faced an enemy who was difficult to combat
⟶ We faced an enemy difficult to combat

This is an acceptable sentence as it stands, but if we wish, we can carry out an order-change so that the sequence NOUN + ADJECTIVE + COMPLEMENT becomes ADJECTIVE + NOUN + COMPLEMENT:

We faced an enemy difficult to combat
⟶ We faced a difficult enemy to combat

(The determiner *an* has to be adjusted to *a* because it is no longer followed by a vowel.) Sometimes, when a modifier of this kind is an accepted unity, the whole phrase, rather than just the adjective, can move in front of the noun.

I bought a suit ready to wear
⟶ I bought a ready-to-wear suit
not *I bought a ready suit to wear

7
COMPARATIVES
AND GENITIVES

The base of a sentence showing comparison will contain two kernels of Pattern 2, that is, ones containing predicative adjectives. There are two main types of comparison, which must be described separately.

Type 1 involves a comparison of degrees of intensity of a quality or of several qualities. The base contains an item COMPARATIVE, which develops into one of the following:

as . . . as
-er than (OR more . . . than)
less . . . than

The outcome will be different according to whether the two nominals in the kernels are the same or not, and whether the two adjectives are the same or not.

Nominals Different/Adjectives Identical
[John is sick COMPARATIVE]   [Bill is sick]
⟶ John is as sick as Bill is sick

90

John is sicker than Bill is sick
John is less sick than Bill is sick

It will be seen that the element "COMPARATIVE," which appears in the base, is converted to one of the three types listed in the preceding paragraph, and any necessary order-changes made. Now, each of the three resultant sentences is rather unlikely to occur in quite this form, but it is necessary to put the comparative conjunction in that way to explain its principle. Everyone will agree that the sentences illustrated are right enough as blueprints, but that we regularly delete part of these full forms before we speak. They become

John as is sick as Bill (is) (sick)
John is sicker than Bill (is) (sick)
John is less sick than Bill (is) (sick)

One condition of the comparative conjunction is that the second kernel must not be negative. That is, we must not produce *John is as sick as Bill isn't* (except, perhaps, for comic effect). On the other hand, if the first kernel is negative, conjunction produces a permissible sentence: *John isn't as sick as Bill (is) (sick).*

The comparison can be made in just the same way if the adjectives are extended by complements. For instance:

[John is happy to help COMPARATIVE] [Bill is happy to help]
⟶ John is as happy to help as Bill (is) (happy to help)
John is happier to help than Bill (is) (happy to help)
John is less happy to help than Bill (is) (happy to help)

Likewise, [John is keen on the girl COMPARATIVE] and [Bill is keen on the girl] would produce a set of sentences headed by *John is as keen on the girl as Bill (is) (keen on the girl)*.

Nominals Identical/Adjectives Different

[Harry is poor COMPARATIVE] [Harry is unhappy]

——→*Harry is as poor as Harry is unhappy
   *Harry is poorer than Harry is unhappy
   *Harry is less poor than Harry is unhappy

None of these can occur in quite this form, and the repetition of the name has to be eliminated in favor of a pronoun, thus:

   Harry is as poor as he is unhappy
   Harry is poorer than he is unhappy (?)
   Harry is less poor than he is unhappy

The second sentence has a question mark after it to indicate that it would not be accepted by many people. Some, indeed, would prefer *Harry is more poor than he is unhappy*. Perhaps the sentence is a little unlikely, anyway, but similar sentences with adjectival complements seem more natural:

   Harry is as difficult to please as he is eager to be entertained
   Harry is more difficult to please than he is eager to be entertained
   Harry is less difficult to please than he is eager to be entertained

Nominals Different/Adjectives Different
[Graham is wealthy COMPARATIVE]   [Neville is handsome]
⟶ Graham is as wealthy as Neville is handsome
Graham is more wealthy than Neville is handsome
Graham is less wealthy than Neville is handsome

To many, these might seem to represent doubtful usage. Adjectival complements are found in similar sentences:

Graham is as pleasant in manner as Neville is handsome in appearance
Graham is more pleasant in manner than Neville is handsome in appearance
Graham is less pleasant in manner than Neville is handsome in appearance

7.2 COMPARATIVE CONJUNCTION OF TYPE 2
Whereas comparisons of Type 1 provide a balancing of degrees of intensity of one or more qualities, those of Type 2 compare the applicability of several adjectival terms. In this type of comparison, the nominals in the two kernels must be identical. Typical links for the comparison are as follows:

rather . . . than
not so much . . . as

The divergence in meaning between the two types can best be seen by comparing, say,

John is as unhappy as he is poor
and John is unhappy rather than poor

Let us now look at a typical development of Type 2.

[The   man   is   unhappy   COMPARATIVE]   [The man is poor]
———→*The man is unhappy rather than the man is poor
    *The man is not so much poor as the man is unhappy

These are merely descriptions of what happens in principle; everyone knows that these sentences never actually occur. To begin with, we know that the second occurence of *the man* would be replaced by a pronoun:

  *The man is unhappy rather than he is poor
   The man is not so much poor as he is unhappy

Each of these can then be further adjusted. In the case of the first sentence, the adjustment is obligatory.

   The man is unhappy rather than poor
   The man is not so much poor as unhappy

Finally such constructions can occur with adjectival complements:

   Shirley is clever at remembering rather than deep in her thinking
   Shirley is not so much deep in her thinking as clever at remembering

It will be observed in all the examples that *rather . . . than* and *not so much . . . as* differ in the order in which they present the adjectivals for comparison.
   Comparisons of Type 2 can also be made by means of the links:

   more . . . than (*but not* -er)
   less . . . than

With such links, the distinction between Types 1 and 2 becomes blurred. Sometimes they are kept separate by features of intonation and pausing, or, in written English, by the use of quotation marks.

Type 1: The man is more unhappy than he is poor
Type 2: The man is more "unhappy" than he is "poor"

However, the meanings become so similar with such links that the distinction is rather elusive, and is frequently ignored.

7.3 COMPARATIVE CONJUNCTIONS† AS RELATIVE CLAUSES

We saw earlier the several stages by which adjectives are embedded into host sentences by way of relative clauses. So, if we start with two kernels, one of which contains a predicative adjective, such a base will produce a sentence containing a relative clause that is a potential adjective:

[I saw a circus] [The circus was cruel]
⟶ I saw a circus that was cruel

We then apply deletions to produce the intermediate stage *I saw a circus cruel. Finally, an order-change transformation gives us I saw a cruel circus. This change does not take place if the nominal is an indefinite pronoun, for example, I saw something cruel.

---

†The term CONJUNCTION here refers to the joining together of clauses. The word is therefore meant in its literal sense, and should not be confused with the name "conjunction" for a part of speech in conventional grammar.

Now, all the comparative conjunctions that have been described in the preceding sections can be used as relative clauses. One of them belonging to type 1 was *John is as sick as Bill is.* A similar sequence can be developed as part of the base of a complex sentence:

[I visited John] [John is sick COMPARATIVE] [Bill is sick]

First of all, a comparative transformation would be used to yield

[I visited John]   [John is as sick as Bill is]

Finally, a relative transformation would produce this sentence:

I visited John, who is as sick as Bill is

Let us take another example:

[I visited Harry]   [Harry is poor COMPARATIVE] [Harry is unhappy]

The first step is again the comparative transformation:

[I visited Harry]   [Harry is as poor as he is unhappy]

And this is followed by the relative transformation:

I visited Harry, who is as poor as he is unhappy

Even more complex bases are needed to produce more complex sentences. Here is an example of a base with four underlying kernels, two of them host sequences and two of them embedded:

[The television set [Stan has a television set] is efficient COMPARATIVE]   [The television set [Peter has a television set] is efficient]

It will be seen that the four kernels (S_1, S_2, S_3, S_4) are arranged thus:

$$[S_1 [S_2] S_1]   [S_3 [S_4] S_3]$$

The first thing we do is apply the relative transformation twice:

[The television set that Stan has is efficient COMPARATIVE]
[The television set that Peter has is efficient]

And now we form the comparison:

*The television set that Stan has is more efficient than the television set that Peter has is efficient

Next, we carry out the necessary deletion of excessive repetitions.

The television set (that) Stan has is more efficient than the television set (that) Peter has

And finally, as a matter of style, we change the second occurrence of *television set* to *one*:

The television set Stan has is more efficient than the one Peter has.

7.4 GENITIVES

Sometimes the base components that underlie a sentence are rather surprising. The so-called genitive forms involving -'s are developed in transformational grammar from sentences that attribute possession by means of the verb HAVE:

Ron has a camera ⟶ The camera is Ron's

The source sentence may or may not have an indefinite determiner (*a*), but the output sentence must have a definite determiner (*the*).

Now, this transformation accounts for the fact that underlying the sentence *I borrowed one of Ron's cameras* is this base:

[I borrowed a camera]   [Ron has a camera]

As we have seen in the transformation just described, the second of these elements can undergo a change, so as to produce the string

[I borrowed a camera]   [The camera is Ron's]

Then, by using a relative transformation, we produce

I borrowed a camera that is Ron's

(The indefinite determiner *a* is permissible here.) Next, a special form of deletion rule is applied, so that *that is* is replaced by *of*.

I borrowed a camera that is Ron's
⟶ I borrowed a camera of Ron's

Finally, a special embedding transformation makes this change:

I borrowed a camera of Ron's
⟶ I borrowed one of Rons cameras
   or I borrowed Ron's camera

7.5 DETERMINER-NOMINALS

A genitive form like *Ron's* in *Ron's camera* may be
called a DETERMINER-NOMINAL. The nounlike qualities
of genitives can be seen in their form (the form of a
normal noun, plus an ending), and in their structural
roles in sentences of this kind:

> *The new president's* wife will be there
> *The old Ford's* was attached to the back of the car
> (Spare wheels are being discussed)
> *A very young child's* wouldn't have developed
> (Tonsils)

However, the genitives are not quite like ordinary
nouns, as can be seen from these sentences:

> The old man's very clever daughter won the prize
> Our new headmaster's very first action was to
> abolish sport

In the first sentence, each of the two nouns, *man's* and
daughter, has a cluster of attached words, so that two
distinct but related units are formed. In the second
sentence, the same is true of *headmaster's* and *action*.
Normal noun sequences do not act in this way. In a
sentence-beginning like *The very fine school concert*,
we cannot separate the two nouns so as to form distinct units. We cannot invent a sentence-beginning like
The extremely old school very fine concert . . . So
this is one way in which the genitive form differs from
ordinary noun forms. Indeed, in our sample sentence,
beginning *The old man's very clever daughter*, the
whole unit *The old man's* fills something of the role
that a single-word determiner would. It is, in fact, sim-

ilar in effect to *his*, which could replace it. When a single-word genitive like *Ron's* occurs in a phrase like *Ron's very fine camera*, it occupies the position of a determiner and prevents the occurrence of any other one. Like other determiners, the genitive has an influence on what relative clauses can follow. In formal English, if not always in speech, a genitive prohibits the appearance of a restrictive relative clause. We do not write **Ron's camera that he bought in Hong Kong is broken*, if the relative clause is to be understood as defining. However, we can write it as an appositive clause: *Ron's camera, which he bought in Hong Kong, is broken.*

It should be pointed out that in modern times there has grown up a construction known as the group genitive. A whole phrase is regarded as a unit, and one genitive ending is added to the last word in the phrase. So we do not normally refer to *Uncle Stan's and Aunty June's house*, but rather to *Uncle Stan and Aunty June's house*. The construction implies a grouping of individuals into a unit. Note the subtle difference between *Australia's and America's policies* and *Australia and America's policies*.

The genitive is often called the possessive form. This is not a very good name for it. In phrases like *Ron's camera* there is certainly a relationship of possession between the two nouns, but in other phrases the relationship has nothing to do with possession, for example, *yesterday's weather, the plane's destruction, the man's losses, Germany's enemies, the game's conclusion, the soldier's death*. However, the name has become traditional, and is not really much more inaccurate than genitive, whose complex etymology can be found in any large dictionary.

7.6   FORMS OF THE GENITIVE

In writing, the genitive forms are easy to distinguish, since they are spelled distinctively. Nearly all nouns (those which form their plurals with -*s* or -*es*) express the genitive by -'*s* for the singular and -*s*' for the plural.

The local club's surfboats (one club)
The local clubs' surfboats (more than one club)

There are some departures from this simple rule:

1. Words that form their plurals by internal change (*woman – women*) employ -'*s* for both singular and plural genitive forms, e.g., *a woman's life, women's lives.*

2. Proper nouns that end in -*s* in their normal singular form present a special difficulty, in that the addition of -'*s* to form the genitive is unpleasant to some ears. There are two schools of thought about how such words should be handled. Some people put only an apostrophe: *Dickens' novels, Charles' shop.* Others add -'*s*: *Dickens's novels, Charles's shop.* The latter seems to be increasing in favor and has the advantage that it brings these nouns into line with the majority and makes an audible distinction in speech. The third alternative of using a different structure and writing (or saying) *the novels of Dickens* may seem cowardly, but sometimes discretion is the better part of valor. Notice that this alternative is not open to us with all

phrases: we could not say *the shop of Charles*, since it is just not idiomatic English.

The problem is increased with those few nouns (not always proper nouns) which have a succession of esses in their normal singular form. Should we say *the rhesus's habitat, Jesus's agony*, or *the scissors's handles*? One reading of these phrases aloud will probably convince you that we should not tolerate any such forms. Perhaps in these phrases the most satisfactory solution is to use *of*: *the habitat of the rhesus, the agony of Jesus, the handles of the scissors*. The only acceptable alternative is to use only an apostrophe after the normal form of the noun: *the rhesus' habitat, Jesus' agony, the scissors' handles*. It should be remembered that this is a written distinction, and that in speech this form would sound the same as the normal form of the noun.

3. Nouns that have an unchanged plural form employ -'s for both the singular and the plural genitive, for example, *a sheep's tongue, sheep's tongues*.

In spoken English, there is the possibility of confusion of even the normal genitives with normal plurals. *Horse's, horses'*, and *horses* all sound exactly the same. In practice, there is very little confusion—partly because the meaning would be little affected anyway. (You might ponder the difference between *the prefects' room* and *the prefects room*.) There is certainly a growing tendency in written English to drop the apostrophe in many expressions where it would have once been used: *The Students Union, The Combined*

Schools Concert. It may well be questioned whether
such phrases are genitives at all, when this stage has
been reached, since *schools concert* is parallel to
school concert, except that one of the constituents is
plural.

8
NOMINALIZATIONS
AND NEGATIVES

It is thought that some nominal groups are derived by transformational rules from the structures of equivalent sentences. The process of converting a sentence-pattern into a nominal group is called NOMINALIZATION. Three common kinds are shown in these sentences:

1. That Gary was late was rather surprising
2. For Gary to be late was rather surprising
3. Gary's being late was rather surprising

The subjects of 1, 2, and 3 have certain items in common. Each contains the word *Gary*, a part of the verb BE, and the word *late*. Let us forget, for the moment, that the verb BE occurs in a different form in each of the sentences and simply represent them all by the symbol BE. We could then say that the main part of the subject in each sentence was

Gary BE late

We could then think of the complete sentences as having the underlying structure

104

4. [[Gary BE late] was rather surprising]

To this basic pattern, we then add any one of these elements:

that
for . . . to
's . . . ing

These are called COMPLEMENTIZERS. The result, after we fixed up the form of BE appropriately, would be sentences 1, 2, and 3. This means that we can start from a single underlying sequence, 4, and, by effecting certain changes, produce three sentences.

But that is not all. Compare the following sentences with 1 and 2:

5. It was rather surprising that Gary was late
6. It was rather surprising for Gary to be late

This time, the same sequence, *Gary* BE *late*, occurs in both sentences, but at the end. Also, the word *it* has appeared at the beginning, in the place where this sequence was before. All of these facts can be taken into account, and sentences 1, 2, 3, 5, and 6 can all be derived from the same source, if we imagine an underlying structure of the form

7. [It [Gary BE late] was rather surprising]

If we wish to derive any of sentences 1, 2, or 3, we simply add the appropriate complementizer and delete *it*. If we wish to arrive at sentence 5 or 6, we add *that* or *for . . . to* and move the embedded clause to the end of the sentence. This movement cannot be carried out if the complementizer *'s . . . ing* has been used.

8.2 OTHER NOMINALIZATIONS

The status of certain other nominalizations is less clear. Obviously, there is some relationship between the following verbs and nouns:

depart	departure
refuse	refusal
discuss	discussion
arrange	arrangement

Some linguists hold the view that the nouns are formed from sentences containing the corresponding verbs, in much the same way as the nominalizations were made in 8.1, but this view has recently been strongly challenged, and it may be that the relationship between the two lists is merely a lexical one, that is, a "word-building" one. The precise operations needed are not yet clear.

A similar problem exists for certain nouns that are obviously related to adjectives in some way:

arrogant	arrogance
pure	purity
anxious	anxiety
happy	happiness

A slightly different problem is that of the relationship between a verb like *to smoke* and the corresponding noun form *a smoker*, or the verb *to bake* and the noun *baker*. This question is complicated (or simplified?) by the fact that there is no verb *to groce* to match *grocer*, and no verb *to butch* to match *butcher*.

Finally, there is the still unsolved problem of the relationship between *John's driving the car* and *John's driving of the car*. The two are different in meaning, as the following sentences illustrate:

John's driving the car didn't please me, but there was no one else to do it

John's driving of the car didn't please me, and I thought he should have been more careful

8.3 SENTENCE NEGATION: *NOT*

If we wish to change a positive statement to its negative counterpart, the simplest way is to add *not* or *-n't* after the first auxiliary in the sentence, where one occurs.

[NEG + The train is running late]
⟶ The train isn't running late
[NEG + You should be going to school]
⟶ You shouldn't be going to school

Sometimes, minor adjustments have to be made: *will not*, in its contracted form, is *won't, shall not* is *shan't, cannot* is *can't;* but native speakers make these adjustments automatically, without thought.

The situation is a little more complex in sentences where no auxiliaries occur. We can say,

The bird couldn't sing
I hadn't noticed it

But we cannot say (or write),

 *The bird not sang
 (As negative for *The bird sang*)
 *I not noticed it
 (As negative for *I noticed it*)

In such sentences, the word DO (in one of its forms) is brought into use as a dummy auxiliary. We have already seen this sort of adjustment in questions, so the reader should be in a position to describe what happens: a form of DO is used to carry tense and number signification, and the verb is reduced to its uninflected form:

The bird didn't sing
I didn't notice it

In Chapter 5, we saw how a sentence is changed into question form when the whole sentence is queried. The auxiliary (or DO as a dummy auxiliary) moves around in front of the subject. We must now note that, in a negative sentence, the word *not* (or *-n't*) makes this movement with the auxiliary (or DO).

John *isn't* going to the concert
Isn't John going to the concert?

In a statement, it is possible to have the full word *not: John is not going to the concert.* It all depends on the intonation and stressing we give to the sentence. However, as soon as we convert the sentence into a question, it becomes impossible to preserve the full form of the negative. Native speakers of English simply do not say **Is not John going to the concert?* but invariably contract to *Isn't John going to the concert?* When it is intended to stress the negation of the meaning of the verb, the question inversion sometimes takes place without involving the word *not: Is John not going to the concert?*

8.4 SOME EFFECTS OF SENTENCE NEGATION

Negated sentences are capable of taking certain modifications of structure that cannot be used with corresponding positive sentences. The American scholar E. S. Klima, in his important article "Negation in English," regarded the capability of taking these structures as the definition of sentence negation. Whether we agree with that or not, it is certain that they are very important features of negation.

1. Positive kernel-patterns, as we have seen, can be joined together by *and . . . too.*

[John will be on holidays] [I will be on holidays]
⟶ John will be on holidays *and* I will be on holidays *too*

Most of the repetitive words can be deleted from the second clause, and the resultant sentence (much more likely to occur than the preceding one) is

John will be on holidays *and* I will *too*

But this link, *and . . . too*, cannot be used to join negated kernels, which are instead joined by *and . . . either.*

[John won't be on holidays] [I won't be on holidays]
⟶ John won't be on holidays *and* I won't be on holidays *either*

When we eliminate the surplus repetitions, we are left with

John won't be on holidays *and* I won't *either*

If we tried to join these with *and . . . too*, the result would not be an English entence: **John won't be on holidays and I won't (be on holidays) too.*

Sometimes *not . . . either* is transformed into *neither*: *John won't be on holidays and neither will I.* What has happened seems simple to a native speaker of the language but is quite intricate to describe. In principle, three things have happened:

a. Either has been "telescoped" with *not* to form the combination *neither*.

b. Neither has been brought around to the position after *and* — a position that was not occupied by either of the source items.

c. The subject and the auxiliary (deprived of its negative component) have been inverted to form *will I*, instead of *I will*.

2. Negative sentences can be extended by sequences beginning *not even . . .* For example: *Our boys didn't win any prizes, not even consolation prizes.* Positive sentences are not able to take such extensions.

3. After making a statement, we often add a tag-question, such as *do they?* or *hasn't she?* Whether we make this tag positive or negative depends on what we have made the main sentence. If it is positive, the tag is likely to be negative; if it is negative, the tag is likely to be positive:

This book is difficult, *isn't it?*
The concerto wasn't finished, *was it?*

Note that the preceding describes a tendency, not an inflexible rule. If the main clause is positive, the tag need not necessarily be negative. We might say *This book is difficult, is it?* On the other hand, if the main clause is negative, the tag will not inevitably be positive. We can say *The concerto wasn't fin-ished, wasn't it*? It seems to me that there is even a subtle difference of implication between a posi-tive and a negative tag on the same sentence. *The concerto wasn't finished, was it*? carries the impli-cation: "I don't think it was, but I am just checking to be sure." *The concerto wasn't finished, wasn't it*? carries the implication: "You have just told me that it wasn't (or, I have just realized), and my question is almost rhetorical." There are similar, but reversed, implications with positive and nega-tive tags for the other sentence.

There are other structures, too, that are typically associated with sentence-negation. The modal auxil-iary *need* is found in such negative sentences as *You needn't bother* and *Hawkers and canvassers need not call*, but there are no corresponding positive sentences *You need bother* and *Hawkers and canvassers need call*. This restriction does not apply to *need to* + infini-tive, only to *need* without *to*. *Can't help* + present parti-ciple is another structure that is typically negative: *I can't help singing*. It would be unusual to find a sen-tence like *I can help singing*, though it is true that people sometimes say *You can help it if you want to*, when they wish to rebuff a negative statement.

8.5 NEGATIVE PREVERBS

The other negative preverbs mentioned in Chapter 4 were: *never, scarcely, seldom, rarely, hardly, barely, little*, etc. When they occur before the main verb in the sentence, they often don't carry a meaning of complete negation, but they do carry some degree of negativity.

They are similar to *not* in being able to associate with the structures described in the preceding section:

> He seldom works, *and* I seldom do *either*
> He rarely buys paintings, *not even* famous ones
> He is hardly a champion, *is he*?

There are, however, certain differences between these words and *not*. They can occur in a sentence that has no auxiliary, whereas *not* cannot. That is, we can have *He seldom laughs*, but **He laughs not* would not be current English.† Furthermore, the negative preverbs other than *not* do not move with the auxiliary to form the interrogative inversion. *He was not sick* becomes *Wasn't he sick?* but *He was hardly sick* does not become **Was hardly he sick?* Yet these words motivate an inversion on their own account (not for a question), in a way that *not* does not.

> Hardly had I . . .
> Scarcely was it . . .
> Rarely did he . . . *etc.*

These inversions are optional, but if the option is not taken, the preverb will occur after the auxiliary.

8.6 CONSTITUENT NEGATION

It is possible to apply negation to individual words or phrases, so that the effect of the negation does not extend over the whole sentence. This phenomenon is called CONSTITUENT NEGATION, to distinguish it from SENTENCE NEGATION.

One of the common methods of negating a word is to

---

†Phrases such as the biblical "They toil not, neither do they spin" are relics of a former stage in the history of the language when such constructions were permissible.

use a prefix such as *un-*, *dis-*, *in-*, or a suffix such as *-less*. We can indicate a negated word by attaching the symbol NEG to it in the base:

[Many NEG-correct answers were received]
⟶ Many incorrect answers were received

Sometimes, the meaning of a statement that includes a negated constituent is similar to one which has sentence negation.

[It is NEG-necessary to shout]
⟶ It is unnecessary to shout
[NEG + It is necessary to shout]
⟶ It isn't necessary to shout

The first of these represents constituent negation, the second sentence negation, but the meanings are similar. However, the similar meanings have been achieved by two different structures. *It isn't necessary to shout* can be joined to a clause of similar structure by *and . . . either*, or can be extended by *not even*, but this is not true of *It is unnecessary to shout*. Also, the most likely tag-questions differ for the two sentences:

It is unnecessary to shout, isn't it?
(Sentence positive)
It isn't necessary to shout, is it?
(Sentence negative)

Sometimes, constituent negation is achieved by placing *not* before the relevant constituent.

I sent it to her *not* a week ago
I will see you in the *not*-very-distant future
Last, but *not* least, I come to our guest

8.7　*NOT MUCH* AND *NOT MANY*

Not much and *not many* can figure in both constituent and sentence negation, and sometimes an ambiguity occurs when it is uncertain which construction is intended. For instance:

Not much music entertained us

There are at least two possible meanings for this sentence: *Not much music was played for us;* and *It didn't take much music to entertain us.* The first meaning is applicable if we consider that there is sentence negation, and if we turn the sentence into the passive, it becomes: *We weren't entertained by much music.* Now it is more obvious that this is not a case of constituent negation, since in the passive the negation has been separated from the constituent with which it was associated in the subject of the active sentence. The second meaning is applicable if we consider that there is constituent negation in the active sentence, and if we turn the sentence into the passive so as to retain this implication, it becomes: *We were entertained by not much music.*

Similar remarks can be made for *not many* in *Not many books filled the shelves.* There are again two possible implications: *The shelves were almost empty;* and *The shelves were full, and it didn't take many books to do it.* The first meaning involves sentence negation, and in the passive this meaning is expressed by: *The shelves weren't filled by many books.* The second meaning involves constituent negation, and is expressed in the passive by: *The shelves were filled by not many books.*

8.8 THE ASSOCIATION OF INDEFINITES WITH NEGATIVES

Certain words have a strong tendency to occur in the vicinity of negatives, and these are often called indefinites. Consider these sentences:

I have bought *some* books
I haven't bought *any* books

Changing the sentence from positive to negative involves us in more than the simple addition of *not*. We must also change the determiner from the definite form *some* to the indefinite form *any*, for we are unable to say (except in rather special circumstances) *I haven't bought some books*. A similar change takes place with the pronouns *something, somebody, someone*, which, in the vicinity of a negative, change to their indefinite forms, *anything, anybody, anyone*.

[NEG + I have invited *someone* to speak]
⟶ I haven't invited *anyone* to speak

A similar change takes place with an adverb like *sometimes*. There isn't a corresponding adverb *anytimes*, but the word *ever* serves the purpose:

[NEG + I have *sometimes* smoked a pipe]
⟶ I haven't *ever* smoked a pipe

The adverbial phrase *at times* can change to *at any time*.

[NEG + I have smoked *at times*]
⟶ I haven't smoked *at any time*

Also, *ever* and *at any time* could change places.

The negative that gives rise to the occurrence of the indefinite form need not necessarily be in the same clause. Sometimes it is in the principal clause, and the indefinite form comes in a subordinate clause:

[NEG + the doctor has prescribed a drug]
[The drug will do *some* good]
⟶ The doctor hasn't prescribed a drug that will do *any* good
[NEG + He was the sort of man]
[He could *sometimes* forgive an error]
⟶ He wasn't the sort of man who could *ever* forgive an error.

8.9 THE INCORPORATION OF NEGATIVES INTO INDEFINITES

When a negative and an indefinite occur near each other, the negative word is often incorporated into the indefinite so as to produce a new form:

not anything	⟶ nothing
not anywhere	⟶ nowhere
not anybody	⟶ nobody
not anyone	⟶ no one
not any	⟶ no
not one	⟶ none

We can see this incorporation taking place within the same clause in this sentence:

He hasn't told the secret to *anyone*
He has told the secret to *no one*

The incorporation is optional.

Where a clause is extended by a complement beginning with an infinitive or a participle, a negative in the main clause can be incorporated into an indefinite in the complement:

We don't expect you to pay *anything*
We expect you to pay *nothing*

However, if the indefinite occurs in a different clause from the negative, the latter cannot be incorporated.

We haven't asked the man if he is willing to pay *anything*
We have asked the man if he is willing to pay *nothing*

The second sentence is an acceptable one, but its meaning is different from that of the first one.

9
SOME GRAMMATICAL
NOTIONS

9.1 TENSE IN VERBS

It has often been said that English has only two real
tenses: present and past. If we think of tense as a matter of formal inflection, and as inevitably associated
with the main verb, then the statement is true. However, most speakers of the language would not feel
that this was an adequate way of discussing tense, for
our notions of it are bound up more with concepts of
time than with verbal inflections. Let me hasten to say
that I think that tense and time are not synonymous,
but the one involves the other. In English, our expressions of time-sense are achieved not only by the main
verb but also by auxiliaries, and sometimes other sorts
of items (such as *about to*).

In our study of phrase structure and transformations, we have already seen the formal arrangements
of verbs and auxiliaries. Here we are more concerned
with the semantic notions that accompany them.
Whether we use the word *tense* to describe it, or
whether we invent some other term, there is a kind of

time scale implied by our various verbal arrangements.

The simplest division of time of which we can normally conceive is a tripartite one: past, present, and future. The second of these is somewhat different from the first, in that it is possible to think of it as instantaneous. All the time there is, right up to the instant that you reach the next comma, is now in the past, if we like to be strict; and all the rest of time after the instant when you reached the comma was then in the future (that is to say, did not exist). So the present can be thought of as a moving instant.

But tense in grammar is not quite the same thing as time; it has not quite the same limitations. There is a grammatical form that we call present tense, but it does not always mean the present instant of time. The form of the present tense, in fact, refers to no definite duration of time; its implication can be long or short. If we say *Joan is cooking the tea*, we mean a vague period of time that we would identify as now; but it probably does not amount to more than an hour or so, and may even refer to this very instant. But if we say *He is an actor*, we are not referring to such a short period as an hour, but to some much longer, indefinite period, which probably extends back into the past for some years, and presumably may yet stretch into the future. Indeed, the sentence may not even refer to his manner of earning a living at all, but may have the sense of *He is a born actor*, and so have a duration as long as his life. If we say, *The sun rises in the east*, or *Three fives are fifteen*, we are expressing what are sometimes called eternal truths. Even if they are not literally that, they are statements that seem to us so permanent that time is irrelevant to them. The form of the present tense, then, is used to cover an expanding idea of what constitutes the present.

But the present tense form can also be used to express both the past and the future. Sometimes a person who is narrating an incident that happened in the past, and who wishes to make his narrative especially vivid, will drop into the form of the present tense. *A funny thing happened yesterday*, a person will say. *I'd just left work, and I'm coming down into George Street, when who should I bump into but Sam, and he says, "Where are you going?"* . . . And so the story continues. This form of narration is by no means restricted to people of poor education. In its more accomplished uses, it can be heard from the lips of even the highly educated. It is essentially a spoken device; but something very similar is used occasionally by authors of novels, to give greater immediacy to their account. It is also very common for the form of the present to be used with a future meaning. *My plane leaves on Monday; The concert is next month; I retire in two years.*

The division of time into present, past, and future is too simple for some needs, and the English tense system has many more divisions than those. Each of the three is considered from three different aspects, so that altogether there are at least nine time phases expressed by English tenses.

9.2 THE THREE PHASES OF THE PAST

As well as the simple past tense, there are the BEFORE-PAST and the AFTER-PAST. Each of these involves the expression of two time-shifts. Suppose I begin a sentence with the words *Last Wednesday at two o'clock* . . . This sets a reference time in the past, which enables my listeners, as it were, to summon up a mental picture of the world as it stood at two o'clock last Wednesday. But if I complete the sentence by saying, *Last Wednesday at two o'clock I had just returned from Melbourne*, I am making a further shift back into the past from the first-named reference point. My return from Melbourne was completed some time immediately *prior* to two o'clock last Wednesday. This double shift of time is what is meant by the before-past. The first shift fixes our attention on a certain time in the past, and the second shift refers to events prior to that reference point. The before-past is traditionally called the pluperfect.

The after-past also involves a double time-shift, but this time the second one comes forward from the past a little toward the present — or really toward the time that was then future. If I say, *Last Wednesday at two o'clock I was about to give my speech*, I have made a double time-shift. First, I have made the same reference as before back to a particular time in the past (two o'clock last Wednesday), and then I have spoken of an event that was to happen at a time *subsequent* to that. And that is why after-past is a suitable name for that tense.

But there are also occasions when we wish to refer to the past in a simple way, without making a double shift; so we can, if we wish, simply make the first reference back to a time in the past, as when we say, *Last Wednesday at two o'clock my plane left.* The simple past is often called the preterite, and what we have called the after-past could also be called the post-preterite.

9.3 THE THREE PHASES OF THE PRESENT

As well as the simple present tense, English expresses a BEFORE-PRESENT and an AFTER-PRESENT. These phases are very similar to the ones we have already examined for the past, except that their reference point is the present. If I say *I have finished my meal*, I am, as it were, reporting what the state of affairs is at this present moment; yet I am referring to an event that occurred (or was accomplished) in the immediate past. This tense is the before-present, traditionally called the perfect.

If, on the other hand, I say *I am about to start my meal*, I am reporting about a present state of affairs, yet indicating an event that is to be subsequent to this time, and so the after-present is indicated. If I do not wish to make either of these special references forward or backward from the present moment, I can use one of the types of simple present already described.

9.4 THE THREE PHASES OF THE FUTURE

Though they are a little less frequently used, perhaps, than other tenses, the BEFORE-FUTURE and the AFTER-FUTURE are quite acceptable English tenses. A double time-shift is involved in each of them. If I say *Next Wednesday by two o'clock I will have landed at Bathurst*, I am first of all fixing a reference time in the future (next Wednesday at two o'clock), and then describing what will have been achieved in the immediate past from that reference point. The before-future is conventionally known as the future-perfect. On the other hand, if I say *Next Wednesday at two o'clock I will be about to land at Bathurst*, I am fixing a time in the future as a reference point, and then referring to an event that is to be *subsequent* to that time. Finally, I can use a simple future and say, *Next Wednesday at two o'clock I will land in Bathurst.*

9.5 *GOING* AND *ABOUT*

The after-past, the after-present, and the after-future can all be expressed by several different forms. We have already noticed the forms involving the word *about:*

I was about to give my speech
I am about to start my meal
I will be about to land at Bathurst

These can be expressed with the form *going:*

I was going to give my speech
I am going to start my meal
I will be going to land at Bathurst

It is true that there is some slight difference of sense between the two parallel forms.

9.6 THE EXPANDED TENSES

In modern times, English has developed what are called expanded or continuous tenses. Their time indications are the same as those described earlier; in fact, they are the same tenses, expressed in a rather different way. All of them involve one or more of the parts of the auxiliary BE, sometimes preceded by one of the other auxiliaries. The part of BE is always followed either by the so-called present participle of a main verb (an active sentence) or by the past participle of a main verb (a passive sentence). The terms "present" and "past," though supported by long usage, are quite inappropriate, and a term like "continuous participle" would certainly describe the function of the first of these more accurately.

Theoretically, the nine categories of time, previously described in this chapter, can all be made continuous, but in fact some of them hardly ever are. The following are quite acceptable:

I had been walking
I was walking
I have been walking
I am walking
I will have been walking
I will be walking

The expanded or continuous tenses are often used when the speaker wishes to suggest a continuity of action of some kind, a frame of reference, in relation to which some other action can be described. *He was buying a paper when the train came in.*

9.7 TENSE IN INDIRECT SPEECH

When utterances are put into direct speech, the expression of tense changes, as follows:

He said, "I'm sorry" $\longrightarrow$ *He said that he was sorry*
That is, the present tense changes to the simple past.
He said, "I did it" $\longrightarrow$ *He said that he had done it*
The simplest past changes to the BEFORE-PAST.
He said, "I have tried" $\longrightarrow$ *He said that he had tried*
The BEFORE-PRESENT changes to the BEFORE-PAST.
He said, "I will be there" $\longrightarrow$ *He said that he would be there*
A simple future is changed to a MODAL form.

9.8 THE CONCEPT OF MOOD

In conventional grammar books, mention is made of four moods belonging to verbs: infinitive, imperative, indicative, and subjunctive. The first is rather different from the other three, for, whereas imperative, indicative, and subjunctive are applied to commands, predications, and suppositions respectively and so distinguish three moods or purposes in the speaker, the infinitive is based on no such notion. It simply refers to the uninflected form of the verb, used without a subject.

The subjunctive in English has gradually been falling into decay for some hundreds of years, until today it survives chiefly in a few types of sentences. It seems to have survived best with the auxiliary parts of BE, as in the expression *If I were you.* In the subjunctive, *were* is used for all persons and both numbers. A few set phrases have preserved a fossilized subjunctive: *God save the Queen, Heaven forbid,* and the like, where the plural form is used regardless of person or number. Actually, it is not very useful to keep the term "mood," and it may be better simply to refer to "subjunctive form" where it is applicable.

9.9 STRONG AND WEAK VERBS

Little overt reference has yet been made to the fact that there are two main kinds of English verbs.

Strong Verbs

Strong verbs are those which form their past tense by a change in the internal vowel of the stem, and which do not add an ending of the /ED/ variety, and which often form their past participles by the addition of /n/ or /ən/. Examples are: *break, broke, broken; bite, bit, bitten; eat, ate, eaten; forget, forgot, forgotten.* More irregular in their formation are *go, went, gone.* Some strong verbs have lost the /n/ or /ən/ ending that they originally had on the past participle, such as *come, came, come; fight, fought, fought; sing, sang, sung.* The strong verbs have been in the English language since Old English times but have been greatly reduced in number. Many that were strong, such as *burn, climb, help, laugh,* and *walk,* have become weak since the Old English period, and new verbs are no longer formed on the strong pattern.

Weak Verbs

The distinguishing mark of the weak verb is the ending /ED/ for both past tense and past participle, as in *walk, walked, walked; love, loved, loved; start, started, started.* Sometimes a *t* is involved in the spelling, as in *burnt, spelt,* etc. Some weak verbs have a change in the vowel of the stem as well: *keep, kept, kept; deal, dealt, dealt; mean, meant, meant.* The great majority of English verbs are weak, and virtually all new ones are formed on this pattern.

A few verbs are a mixture of strong and weak characteristics. *Show, showed, shown,* for example, has a weak past tense, but a strong past participle.

10
GENERATIVE
GRAMMAR

10.1 THE NATURE OF GENERATIVE GRAMMAR

In this chapter and the final one, an attempt will be made to approach a little closer to the technical machinery by which generative transformational grammar is expressed. It will not be a rigorous account but rather an attempt to give the reader some insight into the functioning of the system. The content of these chapters will be harder than that of the rest of the book, mainly because of a greater concentration of unfamiliar concepts and techniques. It is hoped that the book has so prepared the way that these chapters will not seem too difficult, but if anyone finds them unpalatable, he can ignore them and regard what he has already read as complete in itself. Nevertheless, he is urged to read on if possible, as this should enrich his insight into all that has gone before.

GENERATIVE GRAMMAR, in its more technical form, has reference to the same facts as the preceding chapters but organizes them differently. It consists of a series of instructions for creating or generating sentences and is made up of a BASE COMPONENT and a TRANSFOR-MATIONAL one.

Broadly speaking, the base component produces structures like our kernel and multiple-kernel bases, but whereas our account could be characterized as a description-after-the-event (one that shows the structure of certain sentences as a finished product), generative grammar shows us the dynamic process of making sentence structure.

The transformational component more or less matches our transformational description, except that its expression is more technical.

10.2 BRANCHING RULES IN THE BASE COMPONENT

The generative base component consists of three parts, the first of which is a set of BRANCHING RULES. In order to learn what they are, let us recall the first kernel-pattern. One specific realization of this pattern is

My son will be the leader

Let us set the structure of this sentence out in the form of immediate constituent analysis, as shown in the diagram. Now, we can think of a generative treatment

My	son	will	be	the	leader
				DET	N
			BE	NP	
DET	N	AUX	VP		
NP			PRED PHR		
Sentence					

as doing the reverse of this: building up, instead of breaking down. It begins with the label "sentence" and presents REWRITE RULES by which the sentence is ultimately developed. A rewrite rule always has the following form:

$x \longrightarrow y$

This should be interpreted to mean, "rewrite x as y" or, to put it another way, "wherever x occurs, substitute y for it." In the example, the first rule might be:

1. SENTENCE $\longrightarrow$ NP + PRED PHR

Or, more simply,

S $\longrightarrow$ NP + PRED PHR

This rule assumes that we begin with the item SENTENCE, and tells us to substitute NP + PRED PHR for it. In other words, if we want to generate a sentence, we write NP + PRED PHR. An ordinary descriptive grammar might have put it in this form:

SENTENCE = NP + PRED PHR

That is, a sentence is made up of a noun phrase and a predicate phrase. But a generative grammar has rules that are dynamic instructions rather than static descriptions. The next rule might read:

2. PRED PHR $\longrightarrow$ AUX + VP

That is, in place of PRED PHR, write AUX + VP. We would then continue with rules such as:

3. VP $\longrightarrow$ BE + NP
4. NP $\longrightarrow$ DET + N

These rules are now repeated in the left-hand column

and are obeyed in the right-hand one. What happens on the right is called the DERIVATION.

Rules	*Derivation*
1. S ⟶ NP + PRED PHR	NP + PRED PHR
2. PRED PHR ⟶ AUX + VP	NP + AUX + VP
3. VP ⟶ BE + NP	NP + AUX + BE + NP
4. NP ⟶ DET + N	DET + N + AUX
	+ BE + DET + N

The reader will see that each line of the derivation is the same as the one above, except that a new sequence has been substituted for one of the items in the line above, in accordance with the instruction of the rule on the left.

Now we have generated the structure belonging to the sentence *My son will be the leader.* We have not yet generated that particular sentence; all we have done is generate the structure that underlies this sentence and many others of Kernel-Pattern 1.

Each of the lines in the derivation is called a STRING, and each item in the final string is called a FORMATIVE. A branching rule operates on a single item in a string (never more) and changes it to something else.

Derivations are often shown in the form of branching-tree diagrams, called PHRASE-MARKERS, or sometimes P-MARKERS for short. The reader has already seen some of these in Chapter 3, but we will now construct one for our derivation and show the relationship that such diagrams have to the rules. The first rule was:

1. S ⟶ NP + PRED PHR

This is shown diagrammatically in Figure 10.1.

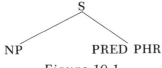

Figure 10.1

When we add the second rule, the diagram is extended, as in Figure 10.2.

2. PRED PHR ⟶ AUX + VP

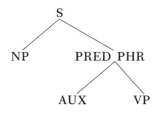

Figure 10.2

Finally, the third and fourth rules are applied (Figure 10.3.).

3. VP ⟶ BE + NP
4. NP ⟶ DET + N

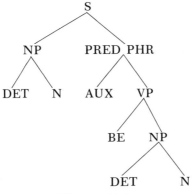

Figure 10.3

10.3 THE EXTENT OF BRANCHING RULES

Four rules have been demonstrated which, taken together, can generate the structure of Kernel-Pattern 1.
In the same way, we could invent rules to generate
each of the seven kernel-patterns. But it would be silly
to have seven different sets of rules, with some repeated
in each set. It would be far better to have one big
set, which would include all the rules necessary to
generate any of the underlying structures of kernel-
patterns. This is, in fact, what the branching rules section of the base is.

Linguists have not yet worked out the best form of
the rules with any finality; there would be some
differences of opinion over the best set of branching
rules. However, the main lines are clear enough. Following is a sample of the rules that would belong to
this part of the grammar. The list is not meant to be
exhaustive by any means but is purely to suggest the
types of rules and their general direction. They are
similar to those we have already looked at, but a few
additional explanations may be needed afterwards.
Here they are:

1. S ⟶ NP + PRED PHR
2. PRED PHR ⟶ (PVB) AUX + VP (PLACE AV)
                                 (TIME AV)

$$3.\ VP \longrightarrow \left\{ \begin{array}{l} BE + PREDICATE \\ V \left\{ \begin{array}{l} (NP)\ (PREP\ PHR)\ (MANNER\ AV) \\ PREDICATE \\ S \end{array} \right\} \end{array} \right\}$$

$$4.\ PREDICATE \longrightarrow \left\{ \begin{array}{l} ADJECTIVE \\ (like)\ NP \end{array} \right\}$$

5. NP ⟶ (DET) N (S)

6. ADJECTIVE $\longrightarrow$ (INTENSIFIER) ADJ

7. PREP PHR $\longrightarrow$ $\begin{cases} \text{DIRECTION} \\ \text{DURATION} \\ \text{PLACE} \\ \text{FREQUENCY} \end{cases}$

8. AUX $\longrightarrow$ TENSE (MODAL) (ASPECT)

9. TENSE $\longrightarrow$ $\begin{cases} \text{PRESENT} \\ \text{PAST} \end{cases}$

Certain conventions which have been used in setting out these rules must now be explained. The first involves rule 2:

2. PRED PHR $\longrightarrow$ (PVB) AUX + VP (PLACE AV) (TIME AV)

The parentheses around certain items mean that those items are optional: they may be selected or not, at will. The reader may be puzzled as to why no + sign occurs between such items and their neighbors. It is simply a convention that, where parentheses occur, they are to be understood as implying a concatenation (+) sign. The reader may, if he prefers, actually put the plus signs in at such points.

Where a rule allows us to select from two or more alternative items, it is conventional to use braces to signal this fact:

3. VP $\longrightarrow$ $\begin{cases} \text{BE + PREDICATE} \\ \text{V} \begin{cases} \text{(NP) (PREP PHR) (MANNER AV)} \\ \text{PREDICATE} \\ \text{S} \end{cases} \end{cases}$

Here, two sets of braces are used. The outer pair indicate that VP may be replaced either by the line

BE + PREDICATE or the line V. . . . The dots have
been put here because there is now another choice to
be made as to what follows V: one of the lines shown
within the inner pair of braces. And notice that the
first of those lines involves further choice because of
the appearance of parentheses. There is a difference
between the choices offered by parentheses and those
offered by braces. You can, if you like, choose all the
items in parentheses, but braces present you with an
either/or choice between two or more items. Inciden-
tally, the item PREP PHR (prepositional phrase) here
must be understood to cover the possible occurrence of
several prepositional phrases in a string. The symbol S,
which occurs in this rule and again in Rule 5, will be
explained later; for the present the reader is asked to
accept it as one of the alternatives.

10.4 A SAMPLE DERIVATION

Let us now take a sample derivation from the preceding rules and show one particular structure. Let us
suppose that we make the selections from the following rules that are shown on the left, giving us the derivation shown on the right.

Rules	*Derivation*
1. S $\longrightarrow$ NP + PRED PHR	NP + PRED PHR
2. PRED PHR $\longrightarrow$ AUX + VP + TIME AV	NP + AUX + VP + TIME AV
3. VP $\longrightarrow$ V + NP + PREP PHR	NP + AUX + V + NP + PREP PHR + TIME AV
5. NP $\longrightarrow$ DET + N	DET + N + AUX + V + DET + N + PREP PHR + TIME AV

7. PREP PHR ⟶ PLACE   DET + N + AUX + V +
                                 DET + N + PLACE +
                                 TIME AV

8. AUX ⟶ TENSE   DET + N + TENSE + V +
                                 DET + N + PLACE +
                                 TIME AV

9. TENSE ⟶ PAST   DET + N + PAST + V +
                                 DET + N + PLACE +
                                 TIME AV

Now, let us convert this derivation to a branching-tree diagram, as shown in Figure 10.4. This is the structure for a sentence such as *The salesman installed the set in the house within an hour*, which conforms to Kernel-Pattern 3.

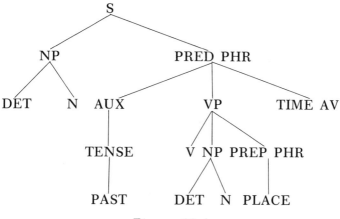

Figure 10.4

11
MORE GENERATIVE GRAMMAR

11.1 THE USE OF THE SYMBOL "S"
In the branching rules of the last chapter, the symbol S appeared in several places. Consideration of it was deferred, because it was more convenient to describe all other aspects of the branching rules first. We now return to this matter.

The S symbols are used in the derivation of generalized bases, that is, the bases of sentences consisting of several kernel-patterns, such as we examined earlier. The branching rules are to be thought of as applying in cycles. In the first cycle, the application of the rules would perhaps derive a string in the following way:

Rules	*Derivation*
1. S $\longrightarrow$ NP + PRED PHR	NP + PRED PHR
2. PRED PHR $\longrightarrow$ AUX + VP	NP + AUX + VP
3. VP $\longrightarrow$ V + NP	NP + AUX + V + NP
5. NP $\longrightarrow$ (DET) N (S)	DET + N + AUX + V + N + S

136

| 8. AUX ⟶ TENSE | DET + N + TENSE
+ V + N + S |
| 9. TENSE ⟶ PAST | DET + N + PAST
+ V + N + S |

Now, this structural pattern would not yet be converted to its lexical shape; but let us here anticipate by saying that DET will ultimately develop into *the*, the first N will develop into *driver*, the second into *it*, which will later be deleted, and PAST + V into *said*. The terminal string above therefore represents the structural base of *The driver said* + S.

Before going any further, we will see how this would appear in a branching diagram. Constructing it is simply a matter of representing the application of the rules by branching lines, as we have already seen. (See Figure 11.1.)

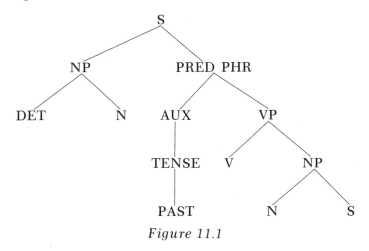

Figure 11.1

Now the second cycle of applying the rules begins, for we can now develop the symbol S in the terminal string, DET + N + PAST + V + S, just as we originally developed the initial S. It is the source of the second kernel or clause. Suppose the derivation of this new S proceeds thus:

Rules	*Derivation*
1. S ⟶ NP + PRED PHR	NP + PRED PHR
2. PRED PHR ⟶ AUX + VP	NP + AUX + VP
3. VP ⟶ V + NP	NP + AUX + V + NP
5. NP ⟶ DET + N	DET + N + AUX + V + DET + N
8. AUX ⟶ TENSE	DET + N + TENSE + V + DET + N
9. TENSE ⟶ PAST	DET + N + PAST + V + DET + N

When this was converted into lexical terms, it might be, perhaps, *The car beat the train.* Our whole sentence would therefore read, *The driver said the car beat the train.* If we now draw a branching diagram for the whole structure of the base, it will extend the previous diagram so as to include the new clause, as shown in Figure 11.2.

The S introduced in Rule 5 can also become the complement of full nouns, for example, *the notion/that we can win, the belief/that all children are innocent.* In the description followed in this book, this S following the noun would also be the source of relative clauses.

11.2 SUBCATEGORIZATION RULES

Suppose that you were confronted with this pattern of an English sentence:

DET + N + PAST + V + DET + N

Suppose further that you were asked to replace these category symbols with words, so as to make a sentence of the required structure. Easy. Any native speaker of the language (who understood the symbols) could do it almost without hesitation. There are so many possible answers that the one the reader chooses cannot be predicted, but let us imagine that you have come up with the sentence *The captain read the message.* Unconsciously, your mind must somehow sort through the possibilities, selecting and rejecting. What shortcuts

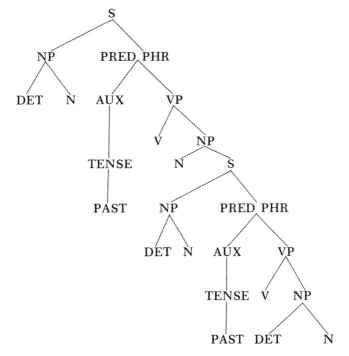

Figure 11.2

it may take to achieve such an incredibly fast answer as it does we do not know; but we are here concerned, not with what actually goes on in your mind, but with the principles that lie behind that activity. Here are several of the things that must be done in principle:

a. When you come to replacing the N symbol with a word, you must choose one that can occur after a determiner and before a verb. And when you choose a verb, you must choose one that can be followed by an object-nominal (that is, a transitive verb). Indeed, all the words must be chosen with a knowledge of which words fit into which contexts, expressed in terms of the other categories. We might call such choices CONTEXT DECISIONS.

b. That is not the end of the difficulties. Having selected *the captain*, you cannot select just any verb that can follow a nominal and take an object. It has to be one that can be associated with a human subject. (You could not choose *permeated*, for instance.) Furthermore, having chosen a human subject and a human-reference verb like *read*, you cannot choose just any noun for the object; it must be one of the limited class of readable things (not forgetting that words like *sun*, *expression*, and *signs* might fit). We might call choices of this kind SELECTIONAL DECISIONS. These are a matter of choosing what words go with what, even after the main categories are known.

Just as you have to make these decisions, so a grammar must contain some sort of rules that will govern these selections. At one stage, it was thought that branching rules of the kind we have already discussed might be able to provide for this part of the grammar, but more recently it has been shown that they are inappropriate for the task. The exact nature of the SUB-CATEGORIZATION RULES (as they are called) will not be described here, partly because they are more complex than this book is intended to be, and partly because they have not been fully worked out yet, anyway. They are probably the least settled part of grammatical theory at present. Still, a brief and informal characterization of them will be attempted.

The subcategorization rules are really a particular variety of transformation rule. They perform several tasks:

1. They attach "labels" to certain symbols, most notably "N." These labels are words like "abstract," "animate," "human," and "countable," and describe the syntactic features possessed by the symbol concerned. Features of this kind are called INHERENT FEATURES.

2. They also attach "labels" describing the context in which a particular category symbol occurs. (Such labels refer to CONTEXTUAL FEATURES.) The context labels are of two kinds: (a) The first kind is expressed in terms of other category symbols. So in the structure underlying our sentence, *The captain read the message*, the symbol V would receive, among others, the label __NP. This means that this particular V occurs in the position before a noun phrase; in other words, it is a transitive verb. (b) The second kind of context labels is expressed in terms of the inherent features described in 1. Thus, the V

in our structure would receive, among others, a label to say that this V occurred after a noun with human reference. This label might take the form [+HU-MAN] AUX___. Our verb occurs in the blank position after the auxiliary, and the brackets enclose the feature that is possessed by the noun that is its subject.

Now, as well as the rules of various kinds, the base component of a grammar must also contain a LEXICON (dictionary), which records the features belonging to particular words. For instance, one entry might be:

CAPTAIN: [+N, +DET___, +Count, +Animate, +Human, etc.]

We would compare the feature analysis of our N in the derivation with various entries in the lexicon until we found one, such as *captain*, that matched. We would then feel free to insert the word *captain* in place of the symbol N in our derivation.

All that we have discussed so far falls within the base component of the grammar, which can thus be said to contain three parts:

BRANCHING RULES
Rules that establish the structure of sentences in terms of category symbols.

SUBCATEGORIZATION RULES
Rules that, as the name suggests, are intended for breaking the categories down into subcategories, by assigning features of the kind just described.

A LEXICON (dictionary)
A record of words and their features.

11.3 TRANSFORMATIONS

Transformational rules are applied to the sequences generated by the base component of the grammar, in order to effect changes of structure only. In other words, transformations do not affect the basic meaning content.

There is an important difference in the ways branching rules and transformational rules operate. A branching rule is an instruction to make a substitution in the previous line of a derivation. It operates blindly, without seeking to know more than the shape of the string. If you have a string DET + N + AUX + V, and a rule which begins AUX →, the rule can be applied to the string. We don't have to find out first anything about the way the string was derived; its underlying structure is irrelevant. Transformational rules, on the other hand, are directed, not at the surface representation of a string, but at the underlying structure, which can often be discovered only by looking back through the derivation.

We have already seen the effects of many transformational rules; our only interest here is to see the technical form in which a transformational rule is presented. The rule for forming a passive will serve as an example. It is applied to a string generated by the base component. The greatly simplified version of the branching rules that was given earlier for illustrative purposes does not contain all the rules necessary to generate the requisite string, but similar rules are used to produce it. Here it is:

NP + AUX + V + NP + by PASSIVE

The transformational rule is expressed in two parts. First, there is a structural analysis, or structure index,

which cites the structure on which the rule works, and
then there is a statement of the structural change that
occurs. It might look like this:

Structural analysis:
NP – AUX – V – . . . NP – . . . by PASSIVE
  1   2   3   4   5   6

Structural change:
1,2,3,4,5,6 $\longrightarrow$ 4,2,3,5,1

There are several comments that should be made
about this. In the first place, the dashes separate the
main constituents, as given by the derivation. The dots
that occur before certain constituents are meant to
imply that other items may intervene, but that these
are not relevant to the rule. What the rule does is shift
the first NP, marked 1, from its initial position to the
position occupied by PASSIVE, eliminating that item in
the process. The other NP, marked 4, is then moved
around to the place formerly occupied by 1. The deletion
of the item PASSIVE is indicated by the fact that 6 is
not mentioned in the output of the rule.

Taken together, the base and transformational components constitute the machinery for generating the
sentences of English and assigning a structure to
them. The notion of such a grammar is that it should
produce sentences automatically. Even though no actual machine might be used, the principle is one of
making the rules as automatic in their operation as
possible. What we have discussed here is the *syntactic*
part of a grammar. A complete theory also contains a
semantic part, which assigns a meaning to every sentence, and a *phonological* part, which converts the

syntactic strings into phonetic symbols to indicate how the sentences would be spoken. (For written English, a similar process converts the syntactic strings into the conventions of written English.) But these matters lie well beyond the scope of this book, and the description with which we are concerned has been completed. Completed, of course, only in the sense that the cycle of explanations has been brought to a close; the complexities and still-unexplained parts are infinite.

BIBLIOGRAPHY

Bach, Emmon. *An Introduction to Transformational Grammars.* Holt, Rinehart & Winston, New York, 1964.

Chomsky, Noam. *Syntactic Structures.* Mouton & Co., The Hague, 1957.

————."A Transformational Approach to Syntax." *Third Texas Conference on Problems of Linguistic Analysis in English.* University of Texas, 1962.

————.*Current Issues in Linguistic Theory.* Mouton & Co., The Hague, 1964.

————. *Aspects of the Theory of Syntax.* The M.I.T. Press, Cambridge, Massachusetts, 1965.

Fodor, J. A., and J. J. Katz (eds.). *The Structure of Language: Readings in the Philosophy of Language.* Prentice-Hall, Englewood Cliffs, New Jersey, 1964.

Fries, C. C. *The Structure of English.* Harcourt, Brace and Company, New York, 1952.

Halliday, M. A. K. "Categories of the Theory of Grammar." *Word* 17: 241–292, 1961.

Harris, Zellig S. *Methods in Structural Linguistics.* The University of Chicago Press, Chicago, 1951.

————. "Co-occurrence and Transformation in Linguistic Structure." *Language* 33: 293–340, 1957.

————. *String Analysis of Sentence Structure.* Mouton & Co., The Hague, 1962.

Jespersen, O. *The Philosophy of Grammar.* Allen & Unwin, London, 1924.

146

Katz, J. J. "Mentalism in Linguistics." *Language* 40: 124–137, 1964.
—— and J. A. Fodor. "The Structure of a Semantic Theory." *Language* 30: 170–210, 1963.
—— and Paul M. Postal. *An Integrated Theory of Linguistic Descriptions.* The M.I.T. Press, Cambridge, Massachusetts, 1964.
Klima, E. S. "Negation in English." In Fodor, J. A., and J. J. Katz (eds.). *The Structure of Language: Readings in the Philosophy of Language*, pp. 246–323.
Lees, Robert B. *The Grammar of English Nominalizations.* Mouton & Co., The Hague, 1960.
—— and E. S. Klima. "Rules for English Pronominalization." *Language* 39: 17–28, 1963.
Nesfield, J. C. *Modern English Grammar.* MacMillan & Co. Ltd., London, 1912.
Postal, P. *Constituent Structure: A Study of Contemporary Models of Syntactic Description.* Mouton & Co., The Hague, 1964.
Smith, Carlota S. "A Class of Complex Modifiers in English." *Language* 37: 343–365, 1961.
——. "Determiners and Relative Clauses in a Generative Grammar of English." *Language* 40: 37–52, 1964.

GLOSSARY

ADJECTIVAL: the name given in modern structural grammar to a word, phrase, or clause that is equivalent in its structural role to an adjective. It therefore embraces adjectives, adjectival phrases, and adjectival clauses.

ADJECTIVAL CONSTRUCT: a type of adjectival in which a single-word adjective acts as a nucleus that is expanded by a modifier such as *very* (sometimes called an intensifier, q.v.). *Very good, extremely sad,* and *rather strange* are adjectival constructs. In this book, a combination consisting of INTENSIFIER + ADJECTIVE.

ADJECTIVE: in modern structural grammars, the class "adjective" has sometimes been rather different in conception from the traditional one, and not coextensive with it. For instance, adjectives have sometimes been defined as words that can participate in an adjectival construct with an intensifier such as *very*. This excludes from the class such traditional adjectives as *five*. On the other hand, adjectives have sometimes been defined as words that take *-er* and *-est* inflections, and this excludes words like *beautiful* that form their comparative and superlative with *more* and *most* respectively.

ADVERB: traditionally described as a word that modifies a verb, adjective, or other adverb. There are at least four types of words that are placed in this category by some grammarians, and the types overlap in their distribution.

    1. The words that are referred to in this book as ADVERBIALS. For example: I drove the car *slowly.*

GLOSSARY 149

2. What are here called intensifiers. For example: I drove the car *very* slowly.

3. What are here called preverbs. For example: I *seldom* drive.

4. What are here called particles. For example: I washed *up* the dishes. I washed the dishes *up*.

Whether we call them all adverbs or whether we insist on different names for them is not a very important matter. It is clear that they sometimes must be differentiated, and so some sort of differentiating label has to be used; but it is also clear that they have certain similarities and that their representatives overlap.

ADVERBIAL: the name given in modern structural grammar to a word, phrase, or clause that is equivalent in its structural role to an adverb (usually of the types shown as 1 and 2 under adverb). It therefore embraces, as well as single words, adverbial phrases and clauses. Structurally, adverbials are located in the predicate phrase and are one of the resources for expanding it.

AFTER-FUTURE: a time reference subsequent to an already-established future reference in a sentence. It is expressed in the tense of the verb (9.4).

AFTER-PAST: a time reference subsequent to an already-established past reference in a sentence. It is expressed in the tense of the verb (9.2).

AFTER-PRESENT: a time reference subsequent to an already-established present reference in a sentence. It is expressed in the tense of the verb (9.3).

ALLOMORPH: one of the variant forms of a morpheme. For example, /t/, /d/, and /əd/ are all allomorphs of the /ED/ (past tense) morpheme attached to verbs.

APPOSITIVE RELATIVE CLAUSE: as used in this book, the term is equivalent to "nonrestrictive relative clause." It is a clause that simply adds further information about the noun to which it is structurally attached, and that does not identify or define the noun more closely.

AUXILIARY: conventional grammar refers to "auxiliary verbs." Should auxiliaries be called verbs, or are the two classes separate? In function and form, they are separate but overlapping. If we separate them, BE and HAVE must be placed in both classes; but, on the other hand, there are difficulties about uniting them in the one class.

BASE: in this book, a kernel-pattern or sequence of kernel-patterns, on which transformations are effected. More technically, the system of rules that generates such underlying strings.

BASE COMPONENT: that part of a transformational grammar which generates the structure of bases. It contains branching rules, subcategorization rules, and a lexicon.

BE: a cryptic way of referring to the forms *am, is, are, was, were, be, been, being*, whether they occur as auxiliaries or verbs.

BEFORE-FUTURE: a time reference prior to an already established future reference in a sentence. It is expressed in the tense of the verb (9.4).

BEFORE-PAST: a time reference prior to an already established past reference in a sentence. It is expressed in the tense of the verb (9.2).

BEFORE-PRESENT: a time reference prior to an already established present reference in a sentence. It is expressed in the tense of the verb (9.3).

BRANCHING RULES: "rewrite" rules in the base component of a transformational grammar. Their resultant derivation can be represented by a branching-tree diagram:

$$x \longrightarrow a + b$$

CLOSED CLASS: a word class to which new members cannot be freely added. For example, auxiliaries and prepositions are two classes of words which rarely receive new members.

COMPLEMENTIZERS: items added to a basic sentence-pattern to form a nominalization. The three most commonly used by linguists in their descriptions are *that, for . . . to*, and *'s . . . ing*.

CONJOINING: the joining together of clauses, sentences, or other constructions.

CONJUNCTION: conjoining. This usage of the word should be carefully distinguished from its usage as the name of a part of speech in conventional grammar.

CONSTITUENT: a morpheme, word, or construction that participates in some larger construction (see also IMMEDIATE CONSTITUENT).

CONSTITUENT NEGATION: the process of making negative a single constituent of a sentence. Opposed to sentence negation.

CONSTITUENT STRUCTURE GRAMMAR: a grammar, or part of a grammar, that consists of phrase-structure rules, that is, rules of the form $x \longrightarrow y$ (rewrite x as y). Although it is not formulated in a generative or symbolic way, conventional grammar is basically a constituent structure grammar.

CONTEXT DECISION: a choice of words to fit a structure, which takes into account the context of neighboring categories.

CONTEXTUAL FEATURE: a "label" assigned to a category symbol to indicate its context in terms either of other categories or of features.

COUNT-NOUN: the term applied to a noun that refers to a type of item that can be counted.

DEEP STRUCTURE: the grammatical structure of the base (or bases) underlying the surface structure of a sentence.

DELETION: the process of removing certain structural items from a sentence-pattern so as to produce a smaller structural pattern.

DERIVATION: in generative grammar, the strings resulting from the application of branching rules.

DETERMINER: a name often used for a word class in structural grammar. It embraces words that were called articles, demonstrative adjectives, and indefinite adjectives in conventional grammar (3.3).

DETERMINER-NOMINAL: what would be called in conventional grammar a noun in possessive case is called a determiner-nominal in this book, because it has some of the characteristics of a determiner and some of a noun. For example, *John's* house (7.5).

DISCOVERY PROCEDURE: a method in which a linguist describes, step by step, how he has drawn a given description of language from the observed data. No adequate discovery procedure has ever been developed for grammar, and Chomsky has argued convincingly that it is unreasonable to expect one, since no other science can provide one either.

DO: a cryptic way of referring to the forms *do, does, did, done, doing*, whether they occur as auxiliaries or verbs.

FORMATIVE: a minimal syntactic item in a terminal string generated by the base component of a grammar.

FORM CLASS: in structural grammar, such as that expounded by Fries, there are said to be four main classes of words, called form classes. They contain the words that are capable of taking grammatical inflections. Most of the words in the form classes would be called nouns, verbs, adjectives, or adverbs in conventional grammar, but the two sets of classes are not exactly coextensive. In Fries's grammar, form classes, which are "open," are opposed to function groups which are "closed."

FUNCTION WORDS: in Fries's structural grammar, words that are not members of one of the form classes (q.v.) belong to one of the numerous small groups of function words; that is, words whose main role is to assist in the structure of the sentence. They are "closed" groups, and, although they fill fifteen groups, there are only 154 items involved altogether, according to Fries.

GENERALIZED BASE: in transformational grammar, a base (q.v.) that is made up of more than one kernel-pattern (Chapter 6).

GENERALIZED PHRASE-MARKER: in formal treatments of transformational grammar, a phrase-marker that contains more than one S symbol.

GENERATIVE GRAMMAR: any grammar with generative rules; that is, ones that are instructions for generating (or forming) the grammatical sentences of a language.

HAVE: a cryptic way of referring to the forms *has, have, had, having*, whether they occur as auxiliaries or verbs.

IMMEDIATE CONSTITUENT: a constituent (q.v.) that is one of the primary structural items of some larger construction. For example, in the sentence *The car with the red upholstery belongs to my cousin*, the immediate constituents of the sentence are *The car with the red upholstery* and *belongs to my cousin*. Each of these portions also has immediate constituents of its own. In the first portion, they are *the car* and *with the red upholstery*. *The car* is a constituent of the whole sentence, but not an immediate one. It is an immediate constituent only of *the car with the red upholstery*. The term "immediate constituent" is often abbreviated to I.C. (2.4).

INHERENT FEATURE: a label describing a syntactic quality, which may be attached to a category symbol. For example, "N" may receive such features as "abstract," "animate," "human," and "countable."

INTENSIFIER: a name that has been used in structural grammars for a word class that includes *very, extremely, rather*, etc. For example: A *very* good friend came to see me. You acted *extremely* wisely. Intensifiers participate in adjectival and adverbial constructs, as shown in the two examples. In conventional grammar they are called adverbs but are only one of several types.

INTRANSITIVE VERB: a verb that may not be followed by an object, for example, *arrive, disappear.*

KERNEL-PATTERN: the arrangement of structural items in a sequence in order to describe the form of a kernel sentence.

KERNEL SENTENCE: a basic sentence-type, from which more complex structures are derived.

LEXICON: a dictionary. More specifically, in transformational grammar, a list of morphemes, words, etc., and their grammatical and semantic features. The lexicon is part of the base component of a transformational grammar.

MASS-NOUN: a term used for nouns which refer to masses, and not to separately countable items, for example, *meat, water, sugar.*

Some mass-nouns can also on occasions be used as count-nouns, for example, *You must be careful to select the right meats.*

MODAL: a modal auxiliary.

MODAL AUXILIARY: an auxiliary verb that conveys the "mood" or "mode" of the action expressed in the main verb. *Can, could, may, might, must, shall, should, will*, and *would* are the items usually called "modal auxiliaries."

MORPHEME: the smallest linguistic form that is grammatically pertinent. For example, *boys* consists of two morphemes, *boy* and *s*. *Hotel* consists of just one (4.1).

NOMINAL: a word, phrase, or clause which is equivalent to a noun in its structural role. It embraces nouns, pronouns, noun phrases, and noun clauses.

NOMINAL WORD: a noun or a pronoun.

NOMINALIZATION: the process of converting any grammatical sequence into a nominal. For example, if we nominalize the adjective *true*, the result is *truth*; if we nominalize the sentence *John plays the piano*, the result is *John's piano-playing.*

NOUN PHRASE: any phrase whose head-word is a noun or a pronoun. More specifically, one of the two immediate constituents of a kernel sentence, the other being a predicate phrase.

OPEN CLASS: a word class to which new members can be freely added. In English, the open classes of conventional grammar are nouns, verbs, adjectives, and adverbs.

ORDER-CHANGE: a change introduced in the order of occurrence of items in a string, through a transformation.

PARTICLE: in conventional grammar, the term has been used to refer to articles, conjunctions, interjections, prepositions, and even prefixes and suffixes. In this book it is used only as a description of words such as *up* in the following: We washed *up* the dishes. We washed the dishes *up*.

PHRASAL VERB: the name sometimes given to verb-adverb or verb-particle combinations that act, for some purposes, as if they were single verbs. Examples are *wash up, take over.*

PHRASE-MARKER (P-MARKER): a branching-tree diagram representing the derivation resulting from the application of branching rules (10.2).

PHRASE-STRUCTURE RULES (PS RULES): rules for generating the constituent structure of grammatically well-formed sentences. Phrase-structure rules, which are sometimes called constituent structure rules, are a type of branching rules, though branching rules need not necessarily be phrase-structure rules.

PREDICATE PHRASE: one of the two immediate constituents of a kernel sentence, the other being a noun phrase.

PREDICATIVE ADJECTIVE: an adjective that is "predicated" of a noun (said to refer to it) by an intervening copula. Examples are: Sue is *pretty*; Bob seems *upset*.

PREVERB: the name given to a class of words standing in various positions before the verb. There are positive preverbs, such as *always*, *usually*, and *frequently*, and negative ones such as *never*, *scarcely*, and *seldom*. In conventional grammar, such words are called adverbs, and in more modern grammars, too, they are often called preverb adverbs.

RESTRICTIVE CLAUSE: a relative clause which defines or identifies the reference of the nominal to which it is attached.

REWRITE RULE: a rule in the base of a grammar, having the form $X \longrightarrow Y$. (This should be read "Rewrite X as Y.") Such rules are used to generate phrase-markers (tree structures).

SELECTIONAL DECISION: the choice of particular representatives of classes that can occur together in a given grammatical pattern. For example, *boy* and *read* could be selected to represent NP^1 and TR VERB in the sentence-pattern $NP^1 + AUX + TR VERB + NP^2$, but *the dog* and *read* could not normally be selected (11.02).

SEMANTICS: the study of meaning.

SENSE-VERB: certain verbs, most of which refer to the experiencing of sense-impressions, are called sense-verbs. The category includes some words that do not really match this description, but that play the same structural role as words that do. *Feel, smell, taste, seem, become,* and *turn* are some of the verbs treated as sense-verbs in this book (3.11, 3.12).

SENTENCE NEGATION: the process of making negative the import of a whole sentence. Opposed to constituent negation.

SPECIAL DETERMINER: the term used for the determiners *all* and *both* which often occur preceding other determiners in a noun phrase (3.3).

SPECIFIED DETERMINER: a determiner such as *a* or *the* which can refer to a specific individual item or person (6.4).

STRING: a sequence of concatenated grammatical items, such as NP + AUX + TR VERB + AV.

STRUCTURAL GRAMMAR: broadly, any grammar in which there is an attempt to describe the structure of grammatical sentences; but the term has come to refer more narrowly to the type of grammar brought to its maximum development in the early 1950's by such men as C. C. Fries and Zellig Harris (2.1). Structural grammar in this sense is characterized by the procedure known as substitution, by which word class membership is established, and by which smaller structures are expanded to larger. The procedures and results of structural grammar have been absorbed into transformational grammar, where they appear in the base component (especially the branching rules).

STRUCTURE INDEX: the structural analysis that is presented as the first part of a transformational rule, and that describes what sort of underlying strings are subject to a particular transformation. (The second part of the rule describes the structural change that is effected by the transformation.)

SUBCATEGORIZATION RULES: rules which deal with subdivisions within main grammatical categories (11.2).

SUBSTITUTION: the process of replacing one item in a syntactic string by one or more others.

SURFACE STRUCTURE: the apparent structure of a sentence, as opposed to the underlying structures that have been transformed to produce it. The surface structure determines the phonetic character of a sentence.

TERMINAL STRING: in the base component of a grammar, a string consisting wholly of symbols that cannot be developed further by the rules.

TRANSFORMATION: a type of rule in a generative grammar that is more powerful than branching or phrase-structure rules. Transformations can add symbols, delete them, make substitutions, or effect order-changes. They operate on the underlying strings of given sentence structures (Chapters 10,11).

TRANSFORMATIONAL GRAMMAR: any grammar that makes use of transformational rules.

TRANSITIVE VERB: a verb that may take an object, for example, *hit*, *read*.

UNIQUE DETERMINER: the word *the*, when it occurs with a proper noun so as to indicate a unique person, place, etc. For example: *The* Murray is a river. *The* Queen visited Australia. Sometimes in formal descriptions, a proper noun like *Paul*, which occurs without a determiner, is said to have a zero determiner, which is shown by the symbol ⊘. In this case, too, it is sometimes said that the proper noun has a unique determiner.

unspecified determiner: words such as *any* or *all*, where no specific individuals are referred to, are called unspecified determiners (6.4).

WH-QUESTION: a question that begins with *who, what, which, when, where, why,* etc., as opposed to questions that invite a *yes/no* answer. *How* is also usually regarded as a *wh*-word on the basis of its distribution, in spite of the fact that it does not technically qualify on its spelling.

WORD CLASS: structural and other modern grammars tend to use the term "word class" instead of the conventional "part of speech." The members of word classes are often similar to those belonging to parts of speech, but the concept of the category is usually different. Word classes tend to be based on position in sentence patterns or on formal criteria, whereas parts of speech were often defined by their meaning or the function of their meaning.

Noun (*continued*)
    82, 99, 100, 102, 106, 142
  abstract, 34, 35, 55
  collective, 55
  common, 34, 35
  concrete, 34
  count, 55, 151
  mass, 55, 152
  proper, 34, 55, 85, 101, 102
Number, 49–61, 68, 74, 108, 125
  in nouns, 50–56, 101
  plural, 35, 50, 51, 52, 53, 54, 55, 57, 101, 102, 103
  singular, 35, 50, 51, 52, 54, 55, 57, 101, 102

Object, 40, 41, 44, 63, 67, 70, 71, 73, 75, 82, 83
  indirect, 69–70
Old English, 59, 69, 126
Order-change, 88–89, 91, 95, 153
Parsing, 1, 2, 9
Participle
  past, 60, 61, 68, 123, 125, 126
  present, 111, 123
Particle, 44, 63, 64, 153
Parts of speech, 9–13, 15, 16, 18
Passive voice, 60, 66, 67, 69, 114, 123, 144
Pausing, 95
Person, 35, 68, 125
Phases
  of the future, 122–123
  of the past, 120–121
  of the present, 122
Phonetic symbols, 145
Phrasal verb, 44, 153
Phrase, 25, 26, 85, 112
  adjectival, 26, 81
  adverbial, 26, 40, 115
  noun, 26
Phrase marker, 130, 152, 153

Phrase structure, 118
Plural, 54, 55, 125
  Anglicized, 53
  non-English, 52–53
  unchanged, 52, 102
  see also Number
Position in structure, 13, 15, 18, 23, 25, 88
Possessive form, 34, 100
Predicate, 25
Predicate phrase, 24, 25, 32, 36, 39, 40, 129, 154
Prefix, 113
Preposition, 7, 25, 42
Prepositional phrase, 25, 42, 43, 45, 69, 70, 87, 134
Preverb, 39, 40, 154
  negative, 111–112
Pronoun, 34, 35–36, 40, 57, 63, 68, 80, 92, 94, 115
  indefinitive, 36, 88, 95
  personal, 35–36
  plural, 35, 57, 58
  relative, 82, 83, 85
  singular, 35, 57, 58
Pronunciation, 50, 51, 52

Quantifier, 33
Question, 10, 74, 75, 76, 77, 108, 112
  tag-, 65, 110, 111, 113
  wh-, 72–77, 155
Quotation marks, 95

Roberts, Paul, 14
Rules, 2, 5, 6, 28, 29, 130–131, 140, 142, 144
  branching, 128–134, 136–137, 142, 143, 150
  constituent structure, 29
  of Latin, 6
  phrase structure, 153
  rewrite, 129, 154
  subcategorization, 138–142, 155
  transformational, 27, 104, 141, 143